Barye; Life and Works of Antoine Louis Barye, Sculptor: With Eight-six Wood Cuts Artotypes and Prints, in Memory of an Exhibition of His Bronzes, Paintings, and Water-colors Held at New-York in Aid of the Fund of His Monument at Paris

Charles De Kay

BIBLIOLIFE

BARYE

LIFE AND WORKS OF ANTOINE LOUIS BARYE
SCULPTOR WITH EIGHTY-SIX WOOD-CUTS
ARTOTYPES AND PRINTS IN MEMORY OF AN
EXHIBITION OF HIS BRONZES PAINTINGS
AND WATER-COLORS HELD AT NEW-YORK
IN AID OF THE FUND FOR HIS MONUMENT
AT PARIS   WRITTEN BY CHARLES DE KAY

PUBLISHED BY THE BARYE MONUMENT ASSO-
CIATION AT NEW-YORK IN NOVEMBER OF
M D CCC LXXXIX

No. 84.   FORCE.
Stone Group on the Louvre.

A NOTE IN PREFACE

France has writers and critics so many and so able that it seems presumptuous in an American to discuss one of her masters. Yet how often do we not find the view taken by a foreigner more suggestive than the opinions of a fellow-countryman! A great artist may be regarded through various facets, of which the one may be not less true than the other.

The volume offered by the Barye Monument Association to those interested in the fund for a monument to Antoine Louis Barye at Paris is the memorial of a very uncommon event. The United States has no sentimental feeling with regard to France as the fatherland, like that which a large number of Americans cherish toward Great Britain and Ireland. Bonds of amity were knit in the past, and others have been formed since France became a republic; but the difference of tongue more than offsets these. Therefore great merit must exist in the artist whose work exercises enough fascination to set Americans on the task of gathering funds for a monument that is to stand three thousand miles away across the ocean. It is often said that art has no country. But when, before this, has a foreign land raised a monument to a sculptor of modern times?

One object toward which this work tends is the establishment of sculpture in its proper place by the side of painting. Whatever diversity of opinion may exist with regard to the psychological effect exerted by the grim statuettes of Barye on observers, it will be acknowledged that sculptures on a small scale, wrought with the learning and skill he showed, deserve more than common encouragement at present. They form the taste of those who buy them, and tend to save the people from wasting

B   ix

their wealth on bad art. The exhibition at the American Art Galleries begins a veritable mission work in favor of sculpture for the house and home.

Aside from its purpose as a memorial of the exhibition it offers the only comprehensive Life of Barye in English. Even the French treatise by M. Arsène Alexandre does not give a complete review of his life and works while it is comparatively scant of pictures. Lives of sculptors cannot sin on the pictorial side so far as abundance of illustrations is concerned. In default of the objects themselves good pictures are needed to corroborate or disprove what the essayist may advance, or perchance suggest things for which he has no room in his work, things he has forgotten or ignores.

For that reason as many works of Barye as are suitable to a well-made book have been given here. Save where printed on India and secured to the leaf the wood-cuts are impressed directly on the Holland paper of the book, its fibre being crushed down to a surface smooth enough to receive the impression. The artotype process has been selected in order to give as nearly as may be the colors of patinas which the cunning of the master has caused to bloom on the bronze. Thus in one sense this is a picture-book. Containing portraits of the choicest pieces in private hands on this side of the ocean, it takes the place of a gallery of costly bronzes. But, many as are the illustrations, the author indulges a hope that readers will not consider the text for that reason a negligible quantity.

In general the letter-press follows a chronological course, but not a rigid one. The main movement is from Barye's work on single animals and groups of beasts to monsters of legend and myth, thence to symbolical groups of human beings, like that shown on the page before this preface. Barye was a painter of no mean skill in oils and a water-colorist whose pictures exert a steadily increasing fascination, because of their color, their child-like truth to nature, the absence from them of all that is petty and immaterial. But the text deals with his sculpture almost exclusively, because therein he was preëminent. His range as a sculptor is so wide that the old masters of Greece and Italy are passed in review without finding a parallel to him.

Despite all this merit, it remains nevertheless a fact that much which has been written concerning Barye is forced and therefore untrue. Barye would smile at its extravagance could he read it. The reason for this lies in the fact that his genius has been warmly felt by men to whom the why and wherefore of that genius were hidden. In such a matter much of course remains and will remain obscure; but there is no need to despair of light. In the following pages certain facts are offered which may account in some degree for the appearance of Barye in our century and in France. Can we see the true color of anything in nature without noting the colors that environ it? So far as possible within the limits assigned I have tried to place Barye against his background. Isolate him and he seems a monster. Attach to his figure the strands that connect a man with his intellectual and social environment, and he assumes his proper colors and meaning.

During this pleasant task several friends have been helpful. The frontispiece by Flameng and the right to use a number of the wood-cuts are due to Mr. Walters. Mr. Lawrence was kind enough to forward several books and catalogues from Paris. I have to thank Mr. Alexander W. Drake for many suggestions regarding petty details of publication, a mistake in any one of which might cost the favor of bibliophiles. Very special thanks are due to The Century Company for the headbands and for permission to use more than one score wood-cuts without charge to the Barye Monument fund.

No. 66.
HUNT OF THE BEAR (another view).
Bronze. Height, 18 inches.

ANTOINE LOUIS BARYE

✦

CHAPTER ONE

I

IT is not by chance that the present century offers the first
example of a sculptor who gave his best years to the study of
animals; nor by haphazard was France the land in which he
appeared. Neither was Antoine Louis Barye wanting in comrades who
showed the same tendency in a less degree, nor in successors who approach
him in the power to express, through the fine arts, the majesty, the
dramatic fire and even the humor of animals.

Speculations on the existence of beings superior to men had been pushed
to great lengths in the century that produced Swedenborg. The time
came for an examination on more solid ground of the tangible inhabitants of earth, ranged below human beings, but placed so far beneath
that few thinkers were prepared to acknowledge any connection whatever.
Buffon had made a taste for natural history the fashion without alarm-

ing the men of faith. Linnæus opened vistas into the nature of plants and in England the elder Darwin seized on the romantic side of vegetable existence and tried to give it poetic expression. Cuvier was sufficiently practical and conservative to escape the hostility of those wedded to the narrower view that looked only toward heaven; but Lamarck first sowed the seed which Charles Darwin and Alfred Russell Wallace have fostered into the modern doctrines of evolution. And because he sowed it Lamarck was rejected by his generation and might still be unknown, had not Darwin, with a magnanimity rare among scientific men before his time, distinctly affirmed that it was his neglected work which gave the hint for the view of animal and plant nature known as Darwinism.

Barye was therefore born into an atmosphere electric with curiosity as to the mental if not the moral character of animals, and before he became of age to handle clay with mastery the path of the century as regards natural history was set. Some thinkers of the past, Giordano Bruno in the sixteenth century and Lamarck in the present, had dared to break down the barrier which was supposed to rear itself impassable between human beings and the lower creation. Barye gave himself to the study of animals with the curiosity that makes of children good observers if their taste for beasts, birds and insects is not stifled. He came to it with the enthusiasm of the artistic temperament and was encouraged to persevere by finding from the works of Buffon, Cuvier and Lamarck that there was a whole world yet to discover, not only for the naturalist, but for the sculptor.

But Barye in his turn suffered from the unpopular line which he then chose. Had a canvass of the artists of Paris been made to decide whether his Lion Crushing a Serpent should be placed in the garden of the Tuileries where it now stands, unquestionably the vote would have been adverse, irrespective of jealousies arising from art or from politics. In all likelihood the naturalists by profession would have been lukewarm, because they might not have perceived that to study animals for the purpose of showing through sculpture that they are worthy of admiration is one way of educating the public. Luckily the group was

NO. 3.

WALKING TIGER

Height 8¼ inches

bought and placed by one of those arbitrary acts which sometimes give an argument in favor of one-man power. Yet for thirty years after its erection Barye was neglected. This came about through a variety of reasons, some having to do with intrigues among artists, others with politics; but the underlying cause, which furnished steady fuel for the attacks of ill-wishers and of persons honestly ignorant of his meed, was hostility to any movement that looked toward a lessening of the gap between man and beast.

An epoch, however, which has made the startling discovery that animals make houses for themselves, reason from cause to effect in a limited sphere, and exhibit many of the lower emotions and affections of men, cannot afford to neglect them as subjects for the fine arts. Birds are found to have more than an ear for music and a power in some cases to reproduce articulate speech. Members of the grouse family enjoy dancing; ravens and magpies are affected by obscure gropings after the beautiful, shown by collecting brilliant objects, and the bower-bird constructs elaborate huts, connects them by arbors, decorates the huts and arbors with berries, feathers and shining stones, and uses the buildings for a sporting-ground. So that the rudiments of architecture and the fine arts are present in the animal creation.

Those who reject theories based on the possibility that most animals choose their partners with some regard to their beauty and deny that such considerations are possible to their minds, will yet agree that the men of ancient times and the middle ages failed to obtain from animal life a tithe of the material offered thereby to the fine arts. It is to Barye that we owe enlightenment in this respect. Against manifold discouragement he struggled for half a century to assert the dignity of animals as fit objects for the chisel. Saying little but thinking much, he was content to create works of imperishable beauty on a scale often most insignificant, feeling confident that in time the world would come round to his view and begin to express, too late, and after the world's fashion, the value placed at last on the work of genius misunderstood.

3

II

THE novelty of Barye's position did not strike his contemporaries in general, though some regarded it unfavorably and a few with the admiration it deserved. From the earliest record of man's appearance in Europe, from the carvings left in French caves by the men who hunted the hairy elephant, animals have attracted the eyes that see better than a neighbor's, the hands that draw an object more perfectly than those of the next man. The energy and despair of wild beasts of prey were reproduced by the carvers of bas-reliefs on the Euphrates in such a fashion that we are still moved by sight of their rage. Until very recently the Greeks were supposed to have neglected animal figures, and the statement may be true of the statelier walks of Greek art; but now, in the terra-cotta groups from Greece and Asia Minor, we have evidence of an ability to model the lion, goat and cow, if not the horse, which redeems the Greeks from even this blemish on their supremacy.

Owing to ignorance of the lower phase of Greek art the workmen of the middle ages copied the more conventional figures of animals and were prone to give them a heraldic stiffness rather than the free action of life. The horses in the battle-scenes of early Italian masters, the lions and horses of Rubens, even the dogs and boars of a specialist like the Dutch painter Snyders, are not such living and characteristic likenesses as we have in the present century learned to ask from masters of the craft. The pen sketches of Rembrandt are an earnest of what we now demand. In sculpture the horses of every famous Italian of the great epoch and more recently would not meet the requirements of to-day, because Barye has set a standard of excellence for the treatment of the horse in sculpture which is recognized by the very men who least appreciate his merits, a standard that has made the difficulty of their task harder for those who were his detractors and rivals.

How ready artists were to accept the popular verdict on Barye is seen by the confession of M. Auguste Rodin the sculptor, that up to the time

4

No. 4. Tiger Couchant (water-color).
18 x 20½ inches.

Avery Collection.

he modeled The Age of Brass, and while at work with the statuary Belleuse, he saw nothing in Barye to admire, but that when he himself struck out a path which has recently raised him to the front of sculpture in France and the scales fell from his eyes, he discovered his mistake. T. H. Bartlett quotes him in The American Architect of June 1st, 1889 as saying, Barye was the 'master of masters who clung to nature with the force and tenacity of a god and dominated everything. He was beyond all and outside of all art-influences, save nature and the antique. He was one of, if not the most, isolated of artists that ever lived. Emphatically original, and the first in the world in that kind of originality, he was himself and himself alone. One thinks of him and the Assyrians together, though it is not known that he knew anything about them. It is impossible to believe that he was affected by them, because everything that he did was Barye. He is too strong to be generally liked even in France. Neither is he understood; he belongs to the centuries, and only after them will he be loved. He is our great glory and we shall have to depend upon him in coming generations.'

We need not accept this eulogy word for word; it is given to show the impression made upon a master of his craft after a thorough examination of a sculptor whom he once misconceived. Perhaps an easier test is the coarse one of relative rank. M. Rodin places Barye before Rude, the sculptor of the high reliefs on the Arc de Triomphe, and ranks Carpeaux below both.

III

BARYE and Delacroix may be considered examples of the way in which artists express in their own fashion the ideas of the century, which are, as we say, floating in the air, but have not yet settled and borne fruit visible to the generality of men. Strange gusts of air forerun the storm. These artists of genius represent the forerunners of that storm of controversy regarding the proper conception of man's place on earth which still rages, although the storm centre has perhaps passed.

In all ages the artist has been the one whose work has glorified religion, but always in a subtle fashion he himself has criticised his employers. The cathedrals we still admire in their ruined and re-vamped state do not at all represent, as many have piously imagined, saintly workmen on the Fra Angelico pattern who gave their lives to labor for the greater glory of God. There were such men, all honor to their lives of self-sacrifice and self-obliteration! But the vast majority were souls in whom too close a contact with fallible men, raised by a priestly office to a level above common humanity, bred a contempt and in some cases a species of hatred of the professors of religion itself.

There is to-day an underhand war between the priest and the man who builds his church, works his vestments, pours magnificence of color through his stained glass windows. Doubtless, could we know all, the Assyrians who carved the tablets of alabaster for shrines and palaces, in which priest and king were offered to the worship of the common folk with almost equal insistence as the gods themselves, felt the same resentment against their employers or their masters, knowing them for men no better than themselves and often far below them in worth. We find this antagonism to-day most clearly shown in the denunciation of Free Masonry by the Papacy.

The tendency of strong artistic natures is therefore toward revolt against the conventions of religion; but it is also ready to move against the conventions of society and of art. They have ever disliked their patrons, the aristocrats, as well as the priests. But in addition to these feelings, hard enough to reconcile, they have in their own breasts a well-spring of eternal life that keeps them in a sense children, and often leads them to actions and words that antagonize the world, prompt to take as an affront whatever runs counter to prevalent ideas. These traits are so common to artists in all countries that to mention them is a commonplace.

Barye was born in Paris in 1796 and felt the second great swell of feeling arising from the French Revolution about the time (1815) he began seriously to struggle against the fate that lay before him, namely

No. 5. ROCKS AT FONTAINEBLEAU (oils).   Lawrence Collection.

5½ × 12¾ inches.

that of an obscure artisan in a workshop, all of whose ideas beyond the ordinary would either be repressed by his employer or claimed as that employer's own. As an artist he could not love conventions; as an artist he was full of the open-eyed curiosity, the love of nature which education of books alone represses in the child. Strong enough in his own soul to break his fetters, he turned inevitably to things ignored and even sneered at by the professors of art in his time. This on the surface. But deeper down was the refusal of his soul to accept for the dumb creatures of God that degraded position as regards mankind which was the outcome of the religions that men fashion on the plea that they embodied the teachings of Christ. He turned to the wild beasts, as in preceding ages many a taciturn thinker like him, and resolved to show the world that in the realm below angels and men there is a kingdom in which tragedy and comedy, love and hate, beauty as beauty, and the beauty that contains terror have as good a right to be noted as anything that more directly concerns mankind.

But he could not fly from men to wild beasts like the old hermits who were disgusted with the world. The artist can not live in a solitude; he creates a solitude in a crowded abode of men, leaving it whenever the mood changes and the sight of humanity is necessary to him. He sought wild beasts just as the child seeks them, by going to menageries and traveling circuses. His was the true child's delight in forms and colors, in that look of arrested ferocity which causes the young to linger fascinated between the instinct to run and the desire to caress the quiet beasts. It is recorded somewhere that he and Delacroix, both students, both beginners, sought out a menagerie at a fair in one of the suburbs and passed many days drawing the wild beasts. This was before the sculptor began to make the Jardin des Plantes his study ground. Both artists have left imperishable results from these earliest studies; Delacroix in the superb Lion About to Attack a Serpent, a water-color in the Walters Gallery and the Tiger and Serpent belonging to Mr. Henry M. Johnston, Barye in the great bronze Lion Crushing a Serpent which stands on the river side of the gardens of the Tuileries.

7

In some quarters it has been too hastily assumed that Barye owes his impulse toward the sculpture of animals to his friend Delacroix. This is not so. Yet of a truth he owed him more, namely the encouragement of a fellow-workman who saw the meaning of Barye's enthusiasm and studied shoulder to shoulder with him. And Delacroix owed to Barye just as much—for the debt was reciprocal. The fame of these two men, whose labors diverged greatly in later life, will always remain allied and inseparable except by so much as in modern times the different branches of art they pursued must be separate. When we shall detect in Barye's water-colors a resemblance with the animals painted by Delacroix we must beware of supposing a superficial connection between the two. Compared with Delacroix the sculptor remained stationary in that branch of art which was not sculpture.

True as they are in many respects, broad and filled with a sombre beauty, these drawings are in the nature of work for a thorough understanding of the beast he proposed to model. Their imperfections are on the surface; below the technical shortcomings lies the power that came of a profound study and understanding of animals in their bony structure, their flesh and hides, their movement. M. Arsène Alexandre gives an anecdote of Delacroix that means a great deal.* Barye presented to Lefuel the architect of the Louvre two water-colors of tigers, before which Delacroix used often to stop in admiration; and sometimes he took the trouble to make a rapid sketch of them. Occupied in a way so flattering to their maker, considering the mastery he has shown in painting animals, Delacroix exclaimed: 'I shall never be able to give the curl of a tiger's tail as that fellow can!' And the truth thus blurted out may be observed in twenty bronzes by the sculptor. No artist before or since Barye has known so well how to render the expressions that the great and little members of the cat family register by the sinuous movements of their tails.

* A. L. Barye, par Arsène Alexandre, Paris: Librairie de L'Art, 1889.

IV

A PRISON is a horrible and unnatural thing, but men in captivity have at least their minds to occupy them; work, books, exercise and even play relieve the tedium of their lives a little. A spider is taught to be the comrade of the prisoner in a dungeon and rats learn to come at his call to cheer his solitude. The wild beast however, as it paces to and fro in its bare cage with nothing to see beyond the bars but troops of staring men, is a yet more pitiable sight. Every now and then the tiger will stop and gaze fixedly, the round pupil dilating a little, as if in a waking dream of freedom in the jungle. Then with a hoarse smothered roar that is a sigh, the striped beast falls again to its monotonous stride, to and fro, to and fro, a movement which some instinct causes it to make so that it shall not die of inaction. Hope exists for the convict and perhaps he is accessible to the idea that his punishment was deserved. But the wild beast knows not hope; each moment is an agony to it because it cannot escape, whereas slaughter at the hands of men or under the claws of another animal would have a certain excitement that would deprive death of half its agony. Pity for wild beasts in confinement also drew Barye toward them.

Pity is akin to love, but to his artist eye their beauty aided pity. What a liquid eye, what a soft chinchilla fur has the panther, what a lithe grace in its big-footed spare figure! No wonder the nations of South America keep them as pets until their tempers sharpen with age and they have to be shot or driven into the woods. The habit of keeping wild beasts as pets is so common that some naturalist has explained the gentler character of the American *felidæ*, as compared with those of Asia and Africa, by suggesting that every wild beast now living must have had some ancestor in that position.

Observe the crowds around cages of the smaller of the big cats — South American ocelots, with their dark rosettes on a tawny ground, black leopards of Java, jaguars from Brazil, cheetahs or hunting leopards of India. Most children and many grown people try to touch and fondle them, so attractive is their look. One often sees the domestic cat, with its strange slit eyes, more dangerous looking than these animals whose life is sustained by slaughter and whose prey perhaps has included man. The lioness often looks fit for a pet, and many of the wolf and fox family are as pleasing to consider as so many highbred dogs. The beauty of color, shape, movement and expression in these creatures is endless, cribbed, cabined and confined as they are. What must they be in their natural haunts, when stalking their prey or gambolling about with hunger satisfied!

It was these sleek, charming creatures, together with those of their kind whose traits are ruder, that seem to have first drawn Barye's attention. He caught the far-off look just mentioned in the caged tiger, and shows it with lifted head and twitching tail, advancing toward an enemy. The male lion too has been modeled in the attitude of challenge, with head higher than the line of the back, anger showing in the curve of the tail. Lion-hunters tell us that when the beast is hunting it carries the head low; this is the case when about to spring, or when watching for game. We find the attitude in a terra-cotta recently discovered in the Levant, where a draped goddess appears to be rescuing a youth from a lion. In Walking Lion and Walking Tiger the sculptor has for artistic reasons avoided the commoner way of carrying the head and lent them the dignity they show in confinement, when their heads come up against the bars of the cage, and their muzzles are held high.

This is the attitude of the lion in Gérome's painting of Christians exposed to wild beasts in the Roman amphitheatre. The painter took one of Barye's lions bodily and placed it on his canvas, being certain that in so doing he was working from nature itself or perhaps was better off than if he took from nature. For it is a curious fact that in captivity the male lion as a rule has a fuller and longer mane than in a wild state, either because our climate favors a thicker pelt or because in the wild state the mane is torn by thorns and sharp grasses or damaged

NO. 7

LAMMERGEIER AND SERPENT (D.... R.....)

in fights with other lions. Here we find Barye declining to go to the extreme of realism. He takes the wild beast at its best, even if in some respects its beauty is really enhanced by captivity.

It must not be imagined that Barye saw immediately his path in sculpture or was at once convinced that a branch which is still considered inferior was the one for him to pursue. Meantime he was passing through the ordinary hardships and discouragements of a young artisan without protectors or appreciators. His father was a jeweler of Lyons who settled in Paris and married the daughter of an attorney named Claparède, perhaps in the matter-of-fact way such things are still arranged in France. And yet time and circumstances warranted something out of the common in this union. Lyons or Lugdun, it will be remembered, was a more important city of Gaul than Paris. A shrine of the old Keltic deity Lug existed from remote ages there. Greek colonists moved up from Vienne and Marseilles and settled the place in historical times and the Romans made of it a city enriched with beautiful buildings. Claudius, Marcus Aurelius and Caracalla were natives of Lyons. Its citizens therefore had the instincts and memories of imperial power like Rome itself, and also the traditions of artisans and artists ministering to luxury of all kinds. Ampère the physicist and De Jussieu the naturalist were from Lyons. But some years before the sculptor Barye was born Lyons received a terrible blow, and that blow came from Paris, its successful rival.

In 1793 Lyons rose against the Convention, and held out seven weeks before it capitulated to the frantic republicans. Then its citizens were slaughtered and its buildings demolished. It was as if the antique rivalry between the ancient capital and the modern only slumbered and the overthrow of the royal family of France served as a pretext for taking the opposite side in politics. For Lyons, being an industrial city, is naturally republican.

Be that as it may, the jeweler Barye found Lyons a poor place for his trade after October 10, 1793, and took his way to the conquering city. As Mademoiselle Claparède is said to have belonged to the *gens de robe*, that is to say the guild of lawyers, the inference is that the jeweler married a woman on a higher social plane. But on the one hand the times were so stormy that women much higher in station made alliances with men of the people; on the other, a portionless bride from the lawyer's guild might be very glad to marry a jeweler in good circumstances. But we know little or nothing of the sculptor's mother. She seems to have left no impression on her son's life. There can be small doubt that his early education was neglected. And the age at which he was put to a trade may warrant one of two assumptions, either that his mother was dead in 1810 or that she did not have the character necessary to secure for her son the ordinary advantages of a French boy's education.

The boy was not fourteen when his father placed him with Fourrier an engraver of military equipments, and later with Biennais a jeweler. With the one he learned to engrave steel and other metals, with the other to make the steel matrixes used for molding reliefs from thin metals.

He was sixteen when France decided to give Napoleon one more chance to recover the laurels he had lost and permitted the conscription of 1812 to be made. The apprentice was taken and assigned first to the military department, where maps in relief were modeled, and then to the sappers and miners. As these gentry used to be selected from the taller and more powerful men of the army it may be inferred that Barye was even then large and robust. We do not know how he passed the next few years after Waterloo, only it is certain that by 1815, while in the National Guard, he was well aware of his deficiencies as an artist and had set his mind to become a draughtsman if not a painter, and that by 1817 he was quit of the jeweler's bench.

While serving in the National Guard he made an acquaintance who set him on his road by good advice, a sculptor in his own militia company whose name Barye always recalled with gratitude, although it has never made a mark in the world. From him he got the encouragement necessary to cause him to make a resolution never afterwards broken. How likely it was that a resolution made by a man like Barye

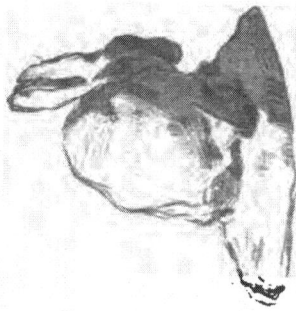

No. 9.   RABBIT ON THE ALERT (rear).   No. 10.   RABBIT ON THE ALERT (side).

Bronze. Height, 1½ inches.   Bronze. Height, 1½ inches.

would be carried through to success, if it took half a century, may be inferred from his portraits. The firm mouth which appears in the lithograph in L'Artiste by Gigoux reproduced here represents Barye at thirty-five. The next portrait and the bust by Moulin show him in middle-age, while the artotype after a superb oil portrait by M. Bonnat is Barye at the end of life. The mouth, which was firm enough as a boy of twenty, grows firmer as the life of the artist unrolls.

About 1816 he entered the atelier of a sculptor of Italian birth called Bosio, a prime favorite with Napoleon I, whose work may be seen here and there in Paris. He made the reliefs and Napoleon for the column on the Place Vendôme, and the chariot on the arch in the Cour du Carrousel, Louvre. Bosio's animals are particularly devoid of naturalness, particularly conventional after Italian precedents; and it may be that indignation at his master's blindness set Barye yet more toward his favorite study. In 1817 he was pursuing his purpose in another direction. Without at once quitting Bosio's workshop he entered the studio of Baron Gros, the painter who drowned himself in a fit of melancholy. Delacroix was not his fellow student under Gros, yet according to M. Dargenty was profoundly influenced by the Baron's spirit, rather than by the results of his painting or his theories with regard to the arts.

All this while Barye had not neglected books or Nature. He was a reserved youth save to his particular friends, and remained a reserved man during life, public and private griefs having, toward middle-age, deepened his sober moods into something very near sternness. Not being given to amusing himself with others, he began to study Buffon, Lacépède, Lamarck and Cuvier, and familiarize himself with the animals and fossils these men described. He studied the past and pondered over the laws, the habitations, the dress and weapons of primitive men; so that when it was necessary to place a sword in the hand of Theseus he chose the leaf-shaped bronze sword which is found in Greek excavations as well as those of western Europe.

Laboring partly for himself, partly for the masters with whom he worked, he longed for liberty, and in 1819 applied for permission to compete for a prize awarded by the Institute in the department for medals. Success would have given him the privilege of a stay at Rome. He was twenty-three, an age when many a clever young painter to-day sees his name cabled to America as the winner of prizes for elaborate compositions; yet Barye would have been overjoyed if he had won so insignificant a competition as that for a medal showing Milo of Crotona devoured by a lion.

That his own bent had not then revealed itself to him we may be sure when we examine this medal, which by some fortunate circumstance has not been lost, though it failed to get first prize. That was won by Vatinelle, an artist concerning whom history is silent, while Barye was complimented with the second. Gustave Planche has found in the lion on this earliest known essay by Barye the germ of his after greatness as the sculptor of beasts. But the critic's imagination has carried him away. On the contrary the medal has in germ what Barye's detractors denied him—the power to express the human figure. The lion is in sooth hardly more than the conventional mask we find on many Greek coins though the tearing of the flesh of the thigh by the lion's claws is well rendered. The best of the medal is the Milo. Both hands caught in the tree-trunk he has undertaken to split with a vain-glorious trust in his superhuman strength, he turns his head and looks down on the lion with the air of a man accustomed to vanquish the king of beasts and therefore unable to realize that his own death is near. He is devising means to kill the lion instead of giving way to despair. We shall find about his human figures in later life the same invincible calm of human superiority.

V

SIGNED and dated 1819 this medal of Milo and the lion begins the chequered career of Barye as an artist. If it did not win the recompense of a trip to Rome, it did get an honorable mention, but that, we may be sure, was for the Milo, not for the lion. There is a coarse work by Pierre Puget (1622-1692) which treats the same subject in

the round. Next year he tried again, but in the section for sculpture, not medals. The subject was Cain hearing the Voice of the Almighty, and Barye's model again showed his power in the human figure. The head of Cain was full of shame and regret while the action of the body was excellent. The winner was one Jacquot, a person now unknown in the arts. For 1821 the subject was the storming of a town of Hither India by Alexander the Great, a subject on which the imagination might revolve freely enough as it is extremely improbable that we know where the town lay, or, having identified it, could by any possibility reconstruct its appearance or that of its inhabitants. But the academicians were of course intent on Alexander as a fit subject for sculpture.

Unfortunately the design for 1821 has been lost, for one might find it interesting to see whether by that time Barye had begun to turn toward animals. Doubtless Alexander was on horseback or in a chariot. Lemaire however took the prize and perhaps Barye destroyed his own work in disgust. Next year it was the brothers of Joseph bringing to Jacob the bloody garment as a witness of Joseph's death. Another competitor named Seurre knew better how to hit the taste of the Academy and Barye did not get an honorable mention.

The Duchess of Angoulême patronized in the old fashion a jeweler in the Passage Sainte Marie named Fauconnier. Such ill success drove Barye back to the workshop whence he had hoped to free himself. In 1823 he entered the shop of Fauconnier, but competed once more — in vain. There was no prize awarded in 1823 for the subject of Jason bearing off the Golden Fleece, and Barye's model seems to have perished. The next year he was not admitted to competition. The wave had closed over him and he had been rudely bidden by fate to remain at the bench for the rest of his life. And he did remain there eight years, during which he modeled numberless objects, many of which were animals on a small scale. Some are lost, being part of Fauconnier's output; others have been rescued, re-modeled and turned into various figures and groups on a far larger scale, thus acting for the

15

latter as sketches. Who knows but that this was one of the lessons of adversity most needed for a slow thinker peculiarly lacking in the superficial quickness which brings fortune if not fame to workmen in Paris, the factory for bibelots and pretty trifles? He had to produce and could not dispose of his time.

Yet besides the small figures for Fauconnier he modeled minute pieces which were cast by Tamisier. Some are pieces one might wear as charms, like the European and marabout storks, the tortoise of minim size. Others, and these are unsigned, belong to the category of reliefs in bronze, like the Lämmergeier, or Bearded Eagle seizing a Serpent, which will be found in the illustration. The energy of some of these small reliefs is very remarkable, made as they were by a young artisan who was kept close to the work-bench while earning his daily bread. One has an eagle with outspread wings exulting over the body of a chamois which he has driven from the cliff. The air of defiance and triumph in the little head is splendid; the wings are treated in a novel and audacious fashion. Hunting dogs at their work and running deer are found on still other bronze placques of this period.

In these the workmanship is not broad as yet, but they are rendered with a decision that leaves nothing to be desired. The stork standing on a tortoise probably belongs to a later period when he dared to sacrifice details in order to obtain the due effect of masses. The charming rabbits and hares too, as well as the Seated Cat, seem to speak of a more mature period. But though minute in size the figures he made while with Fauconnier have each an individuality. And they show whither his taste for natural history was taking him. At the same period he was assiduously frequenting the Jardin des Plantes for the lessons in anatomy taught there. He visited the dog market to study hunting and other dogs, so that in later life he knew the different airs of the badger-hound, of late a fashionable pet, the mastiff, the pointer, setter and retriever, and fixed them in bronze. To the horse mart he hied when a spare hour could be had, in order to perfect his eye in the

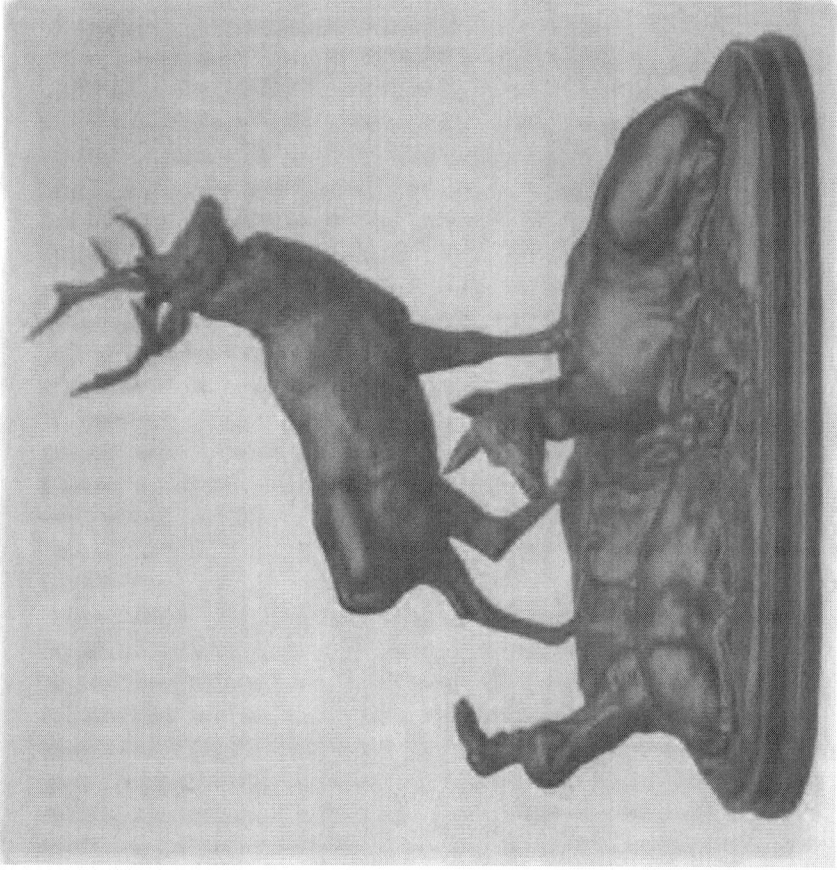

NO. 15.

RED DEER OF EUROPE, HART, HIND AND FAWN

Height 9 inches

'true look of that friend of man which man so rarely understands how to draw or paint or carve properly, that is to say, with the true movement and air of the horse. How much he profited by these studies we shall find when we come to examine his equestrian groups.

But Barye knew that in sculpture a living could be won only by modeling human beings, so we find an entry in the Salon of 1827 of a bust of a young man and another of a young woman by the student of beasts. But these were not destined to award him that triumph among his fellow students and the genuine amateurs which always precedes the recognition of a new genius. It was not till the Salon of 1831, when he was married and a father, that he made his first success. To that Salon he sent a full length Saint Sebastian in terracotta, concerning which a critic (Stendhal) remarked with satisfaction that at least here was a sculptor who did not make legs like a couple of radishes! He also showed the sketch-model of a bear and a group of different animals. But what gained him applause and criticism and the more durable meed of a Second Medal was the Tiger Devouring a Gavial of the Ganges. With this beautiful work, which was bought for the Luxembourg and is now in the Louvre, Barye was at last launched as the greatest sculptor of animals the world has known.

What struck the public and those artists in whom indulgence in a respect for tradition had not mortified the capacity to understand the original, was the passion in the animals. Only sculptors could estimate the modeling, and most of them were too strongly biased in another direction to speak out in praise. But the critics and the public felt the spark of truth that shone through this little work. How relentless are the big paws which have seized the lizard; with what ferocity are the tiger's jaws buried in its flesh! The hind feet of the cat show sympathetically their claws, and the tail writhes with the pleasure not merely of eating but of destroying life. For the tiger, more than any other carnivorous beast, has the ill fame of killing for the love of it rather than for food alone.

3

17

The composition of this group is worth a thought. The tail of the crocodile wound round the tiger's neck, and its body turned toward its destroyer as the jaws vainly snap, form with the tiger a compact group that displays a very attractive outline of its own. Judged as a painting, the design might be called too artfully composed, but in a bronze this artfulness is proper. The trait of composing well was evident thus early in Barye, and though we shall find occasions when he was less happy in this regard, because he felt the need of more natural positions, it is a quality that he possessed to the last. It may be noted that the design and execution are alike. Both are far more precise and deliberate than in his later works.

VI

WITH the fame that was won by this group began his troubles. He left Fauconnier and set up for himself. Two things were inevitable as soon as it appeared that a new sculptor was at hand, but more particularly that a new line of work in sculpture was opening. One was an instinctive, unconscious opposition from those who had been taught to revere the art of the past, the literature of the past, the politics of the past, and that religion against which the Revolution had sinned so cruelly. The other was that conscious and intentional opposition which forms the main burden of complaint for the French writers on Barye. To read them one might suppose that he was the objective of cabals and conspiracies, under the attacks of which he languished for years unable or unwilling to show anything in the Salon. All this seems greatly exaggerated, very unnatural, almost impossible. It had comparatively little to do with Barye's career until he became very much in favor with the heads of the State; then, of course, mud was thrown at Barye which was meant for his employers. But the main difficulty lay not in persons or cabals, it lay in the intolerance of literary minds and artists, and in the sensitiveness of religious persons to anything that smacked of novelty. To them, still quaking

No. 16. TIGER DEVOURING GAVIAL OF GANGES.

Bronze. Height, 7½ inches.

with the memories of the Revolution, the grand style, namely the style consecrated by tradition, was the only one for literature and art; those who impugned tradition roused a fury in their breasts which allied itself to piety and caused much the same violence that the true believer, secure in his certainty that every other thinker is the child of the devil, shows to a fellowman who is not of his persuasion. Where most of Barye's biographers fail is in the statement or the insinuation that he suffered from dishonest opposition. In these early years his opponents were as honest as the Turk who puts Jew, Christian and Persian sectary to the sword, or the Catholic who consigns a heretic to the flames.

There is no beast so cruel as man when he is persuaded that he alone knows everything and contains in himself all the good in the world. Barye in fact was a fore-fighter of the great army of science in the field of art and for many years was a martyr to his artistic faith. Neglect of this point, which was brought out more briefly in an article in The Century Magazine of New York,* has caused subsequent writers on Barye to re-echo the complaints of the earlier admirers of the sculptor, who were scarcely in the proper position to estimate forces only visible to the men of to-day with the retrospect of the century behind them. We must try to regard Barye's misfortunes as due more to the situation and less to personal hatreds and rivalries; more to his environment and less to any special injustice directed against himself. Had he been able to realize this more clearly it would have spared him much bitterness and perhaps been the means of gaining him a hearing in the middle term of his physical and mental powers instead of toward the end of life. That would have been a gain in glory to France. She has made too little use of a genius such as comes but once in centuries.

But it is a satisfaction to reflect that in 1831 at the age of thirty-five Barye had already made so much mark on the world that his work was the occasion for a great deal of generous and acute criticism as well as much violent rebuke. While the ferocity of his tiger startled and dismayed theorists and devotees of artistic red-tape, its splendid life and

* See The Century Magazine for February, 1886, by Henry Eckford (C. de Kay).

remorseless truth to nature gave to others that mental gooseflesh which tells them that they stand before a work of genius, whether it be a carved cherry-pit or a Colossus of Rhodes.

Gustave Planche was then his admirer and remained steadfast to his early views. In the volume on the Salon written by him the cut that shows Barye's Tiger Devouring a Gavial was cut after the pen and ink drawing by Barye. It is strikingly direct and simple, recalling the drawing of William Blake, but not Blake's animals. There is a grandeur about the little sketch which catches the eye at once. Barye indeed tried his hand at a number of things. His drawings preparatory to the clay model are interesting for their patient workmanship and bigness. His water-colors are in some cases superb, in many cases fine, and always individual. Examine the wood-cut after the water-color of a tiger couchant and imagine it colored in good strong yellows. His oils are sometimes muddy, or have become so with time, but among them are capital paintings of deer and other beasts on a small scale, as well as landscapes like that in the illustration. He engraved his own groups on stone, and occasionally etched the copper as in the Stag Seized by a Cougar, here reproduced on wood. He was many-sided, and his long apprenticeship to jewelers gave him a practical knowledge of the means to achieve perfection in statuettes which other sculptors lacked.

VII

THE field that was being marked out for Barye by circumstances and natural bent offers practical difficulties which nothing can entirely overcome. Fascinated by the grace and terrible charm of the cat-like animals, he had to portray them in bronze, a rather stern uncompromising material that does not lend itself to the imitation of fur without a great deal of artistic effort. But it is in accord with an artistic nature to seek a difficult mode of expressing itself. When this material is properly treated it has a sober magnificence no other metal can show. Gold is not a happy medium for large pieces; silver is better than gold but not half

No. 17. STAG SEIZED BY PANTHER (etching by Barye).

so fine as bronze. Iron has the great advantages of flowing better than most metals, entering every cranny of the mold and contracting very little when it cools. But iron requires a very great heat to melt it; moreover it rusts, and fashion has not yet set its stamp on that metal. But having determined on bronze, partly because its warm sober solid look appealed to his own character, partly because bronzes have been the fashion these many centuries among amateurs, the question arose how to imitate color in bronze.

With regard to the large cats it is a matter of no ordinary moment. Thus the leopard *(Felis pardus)* of Asia and Africa has a skull proportioned exactly the same as the lion. Now the male lion, provided the ordinary variety is sculptured, can be told by its mane. But how is the lioness to be distinguished from the leopard, when the material is bronze and there is nothing to show clearly the relative sizes of the beasts? A painting shows at once the difference provided the leopard is of the spotted variety. But even in paintings taken from the life the leopard would not always have spots. For without speaking of the black leopards of Southern India and Java or the snow leopard which bleaches out almost to ivory white, there are leopards of colors running the gamut between black and white on which the spots are very difficult to see. So that even in a painting a leopard might be mistaken for a lioness.

The tiger again is not readily known from the lioness if no color is allowed, for the characteristic difference lies in the stripes of the tiger. In our own land a small jaguar is difficult to distinguish from the ocelot and even in its markings is very like the spotted leopards of the old world. The latter's markings on back and sides are generally in broken rings. The jaguar's are rosettes formed of blackish petals or spots with a central spot. The jaguar is also said to be lower-built and more powerful looking than the leopard, while the latter stands higher on its legs and has a more graceful carriage. But in animals that vary so much in shape as well as coloration in the same litter it is hard to establish any hard and fast rule. The American puma or cougar, called by the European name of panther, and sometimes by trappers mountain-

21

lion or American tiger, is not spotted as a rule in the adult state; its cubs are spotted. It is commonly of a solid fawn color with white belly, yet black individuals have been killed. Some naturalists think that it can be distinguished from a jaguar in which the rosettes are obscure by its longer tail and by the fact that the jaguar has relatively a broader head. But these distinctions are not always trustworthy. They are inconspicuous enough when the beast is done into clay, marble or bronze.

Hence arises a difficulty in deciding which great cat Barye meant in a given group; for it may as well be premised that most of the catalogues, essays and lives of Barye and his works err more or less flagrantly in the nomenclature of animals.

In the first place our guide is the other animal with which the cat is in conflict, supposing the group to be one of the vast number of combats. If that animal belongs to America its assailant can not be lion, tiger or true leopard. If it is an elephant examine the ears, brow and back to see whether it is the Asian or the African. The Asian elephant has relatively small ears and tusks compared with the African; its back is curved upwards and its brow is straight, while the African elephant has a brow curved outward and a hollow back.

An elk or as we call it a moose, has so wide a range that it may be attacked by a North American, or a North European, or North Asian beast of prey. Doubtless even the tiger roams in summer through China far enough north to seize an elk in Mongolia. Distinctions in the deer tribes are yet more difficult. Besides the moose we have the Wapiti or American elk *(Cervus Canadensis)* the common deer *(Cervus*

No. 86.

ELEPHANT OF SENEGAL RUNNING.
Bronze. Height, 5¼ inches.

22

NO 18.

OCELOT AND HERON

Height 5¼ inches

Virginianus) and the black-tailed deer of Missouri, so called, which are all larger animals than the stag of the red deer of Europe. The moose or elk of both continents we tell by its heavy muzzle and great spade-shaped antlers; the American elk by its heavy antlers, not palmated; and our common stag by its relatively light head of horns compared with the body. The red deer of Europe supplies the common hart of illustrations, varying greatly in the number of points to its antlers, from three or more to twelve, when it is a 'royal stag' in Scotland, but often showing twice or thrice that number in Eastern Europe. The fallow deer is a quarter smaller; the buck may be distinguished in art from the red deer by its palmated antlers when three years old. This is the French *daim*, female *daine*. It is kept in deer forests. But in Great Britain and Ireland the commoner inhabitant of private parks is the charming little roe deer, the buck of which is only about two feet high at the shoulder, though some owners possess large herds of the fallow deer also. In all these animals the male alone carries horns and as a rule he sheds them once a year.

These details may be of use to owners of bronzes by Barye who have lost the names attaching to them or have received mistaken names for them. He was careful as a rule not to bring together animals that live far apart, but in some cases like that of the two bears fighting (1833) the scene is the bear-pit rather than the forest and the fighters are from America and India. Sometimes he helps us out by certain artifices that do not detract from the dignity of the bronze. Thus the tiger is generally set apart from lioness or panther by the stripes Barye has indicated by channels on the bronze. His leopard is in some cases distinguished by broken rings over its back and sides. An alligator can be told from a crocodile by its proportions, having a much shorter head and blunter snout and its hind feet very little webbed. With the great snakes the distinctions are hard to observe. True boa constrictors only exist in South America. Where the animal in contact with a constrictor is of an African species we may understand the python or rock snake of that land which does not equal in size the anaconda of Brazil.

CHAPTER TWO

I

THE quarrel between the old and the new had reached a head in 1830. No one, but least of all the artists and young artisans of Paris who thronged the cafés and lived an out-door Latin life we can hardly realize, could escape the excitement. We have seen how Barye took from the scientific stir of his age the tendency toward a branch of sculpture overlooked by others and despised by amateurs and art-critics. We may fairly discover in the turbulence of this epoch the origin of Barye's predilection for combats between animals, his apparent love of carnage. The certainty of the Struggle for Existence toward which science was groping must have been the deeper influence; the violence of party strife and the clash of old beliefs and new gave the more superficial impulse.

It was something very different from the love of a fight which keeps up the existence of cock-fights, dog-fights and even bear-baitings in America, and of bull-fights in Spain and South America. One may

24

No. 19.   A. L. BARYE AT 35; after a lithograph by Gigoux.

say that in Barye's case it was even a different thing from the fashion among French painters to devise scenes of martyrdom in which blood and torn limbs are far more prominent than is needful. A nearer analogy would be the bestiaries or beast-books of the mediævals in which, under the disguise of animals, human beings were satirized. Barye was not a satirist, fortunately for the prolonged enjoyment of his works, unfortunately for his immediate fame and fortunes; but he had his own way of reflecting in sculptures the ideas of the period, a far higher and more artistic way, it need hardly be said, than if, as a professed satirist, he had crudely and boldly attempted to hold the mirror up to the world.

It was borne along these two main currents, the scientific and the sociological, that the young assistant of a jeweler drove onward to his appointed task. A smaller artist but a bolder satirist might have typified the classicist as the hide-bound Crocodile and the Romantic School as the Tiger which held its old enemy in its powerful young embrace and intended never to loosen its hold. But we get no inkling that such was Barye's purpose when he modeled the group. If he had any such idea he was wise enough to know that in reward for a temporary notoriety he would be abused by the one party and soon forgot by the other. And he may have reasoned that in such allusions there is always a certain crudeness when they occur in plastic art, being better fitted for literature. When they do appear in painting and sculptures they are practised by unbalanced men like Wiertz of Brussels.

There was temptation to attach to his great success of 1833 a meaning of somewhat similar nature, namely his Lion Crushing a Serpent, which was at the Salon of that year and fixed forever the name of Barye as the greatest of *animaliers*. There is a shade of contempt in that word which we would not feel in English, because in French 'animal' is a somewhat abusive term when applied to man, analogous to the vulgar use among the Germans of the words Ochs, Rind, Vieh, Schaf for the minor terms of opprobrium during anger, and to our vulgarisms in calling people donkey or ass. Thus Barye was an *animalier* because he made so many statues of beasts, but the persons who called him so always meant it in an injurious sense, as a taunt rather than a definition. But there is this always to remember. A taunting name is often taken up by those to whom it is applied and made the symbol of the ideal toward which they strive and the glory of their party. Such were and are the Beggars of the Netherlands, the Tories of Ireland, the Mugwumps of recent American politics. So the word *animalier* has through Barye become almost a title of distinction and would be in all likelihood accepted without a murmur by Frémiet and Cain in France, Edward Kemeys and Paul Bartlett in America, were it not that the term also implies and might by some be thought to imply a lack of power to express the human figure.

The year 1833 was the turning-point of Barye's career, if we regard 1831 with its superb Tiger Devouring a Gavial as the point when his steady ill-luck made a pause. Extraordinary creative life possessed him at this period, so that he let the world see too many of his pieces at once, and thus occasioned the very natural thought that works of art, produced with apparent ease in such profusion, could not be as valuable as sculpture slowly wrought. In 1832 he exhibited in plaster the group that was to change his fate from a youth of marked promise to a sculptor either famous or notorious as the case might be. It was the Lion Crushing a Serpent, placed later in bronze on the Avenue des Feuillants in the gardens of the Tuileries. The Minister of the Interior owned at this time a proof of the same group, which differs in essential particulars from the public statue and yet is not the little study with the paw of the lion raised to strike. No second was ever made.

The year before (1831) Barye was still casting bronze bas-reliefs of small size, generally square, which are apparently designed for ornaments to clocks or pieces of furniture. At the time they had no higher purpose, whilst now they are carefully framed as works of art and fetch very respectable sums in the market when they can be had authentic. Such are the profile leopard, panther, running stag, and genet-cat dragging bird, each of the four signed and dated 1831.

26

NO. 20.

HART SEIZED BY TWO SCOTCH HOUNDS

Height 17 inches

It may be noted here that as late as 1847 he was producing small bronzes, avowedly for ornamenting the clocks of offices and private houses; some merely as bronzes to lay on the top of a clock, others to affix to the front and sides. By the year 1832 he had become a favorite with the Duke of Orleans, heir apparent to the throne.

The display that he made in 1833 was so large and varied that nobody could overlook its importance, everybody had to come out with an opinion for or against the sculptor. When reading the jeremiads of French admirers we must never forget the situation. Napoleon the Great had been in many ways an antagonist, if not a traitor to the ideas of democracy to which he owed his elevation. A parvenu to the throne, he had to force the exclusive ranks of kings, and once an emperor, he had to build up again the structure of society that permits an emperor of the old kind to exist in safety. The aristocratic revivals by Napoleon were endless. Beginning with his own consort and the fabric of his court, it extended from the social fabric directly to the artistic world, because the latter depends immediately upon the former. Precedents to sanction what he had done might be found in the careers of Julius Cæsar, for instance, or of Alexander the Great. It was no wonder then, that during his reign literature and art should be profoundly encouraged to revert to the ancients, and that all his power was thrown to the advantage of those who looked to the past, but against innovators who were inspired by the scientific air of the age in which they lived. His brutal treatment of the great naturalist Lamarck is a case in point.

Barye's time fell in with that of other men who in literature and art as well as politics gave their lives and sometimes their blood to the struggle against a tyranny which began again under Napoleon I, but by no means ceased with his consignment to the peak of St. Helena. When therefore in the Journal des Débats M. Délescluze ranked the Tiger and Gavial of 1831 above the works of Marochetti it was a heresy sufficiently grave; but when he also affirmed that it surpassed the work sent by David d'Angers, the celebrated and justly celebrated sculptor David, amateurs felt that if this were true an artistic earthquake was at hand in sculpture. We may be sure however that the greater number of them set the remark down to the same fanaticism, sprung of the politics of the time, that affected to admire the frantic daubs of Delacroix. An earthquake nevertheless it was; a forerunner of the heavier shock of 1833.

The Salon of that year accepted the vigorous statuette of a stag borne down by two Scotch hounds, the Cavalier of the Fifteenth Century, and the equestrian King Charles VI Frightened in the Forest of Mans, pieces that mark the width of Barye's range and in all probability earned for him the patronage of yet other great persons whose favor was not always to his advantage, given the jealousy which the democrats felt for pretenders and heirs to the throne. The Charles VI was cast in bronze by the wax process for Princess Marie of Orleans. He also sent a bust of the Duke of Orleans.

The stag chase appealed to the aristocracy who, even under the new republic, preserve the traditions of the hunt in a land that seems to the tourist so highly cultivated that there could scarcely exist anything to be hunted larger or more ferocious than a hare. As a matter of fact not only the stag but the wild boar is hunted in France, the wolf exists and the bear is not unknown, neither is the Alpine goat.

But these were not the most important sendings of Barye that year. There was the charming little Elephant of Asia, a dead gazelle which brought tears into the eyes of sensitive persons, a bear of the Alps and a Russian bear, a combat between a Bruin of India and one of our American black bears, and a magnificent little statuette in plaster of a horse of powerful breed, not a wild variety, upon whose back a lion has alighted with a spring, all of the action of which is told in its flying flanks and tail. There was a lion in plaster and a bear overthrown by mastiffs shown in the later illustrations here.

Barye was but thirty-seven, yet here was the whole gamut of his genius struck with a power and furious vigor, with a gentleness and humor, with a tender sentiment in the dead gazelle that moved men to tears, with a knowledge of mediæval dress rare among antiquarians of

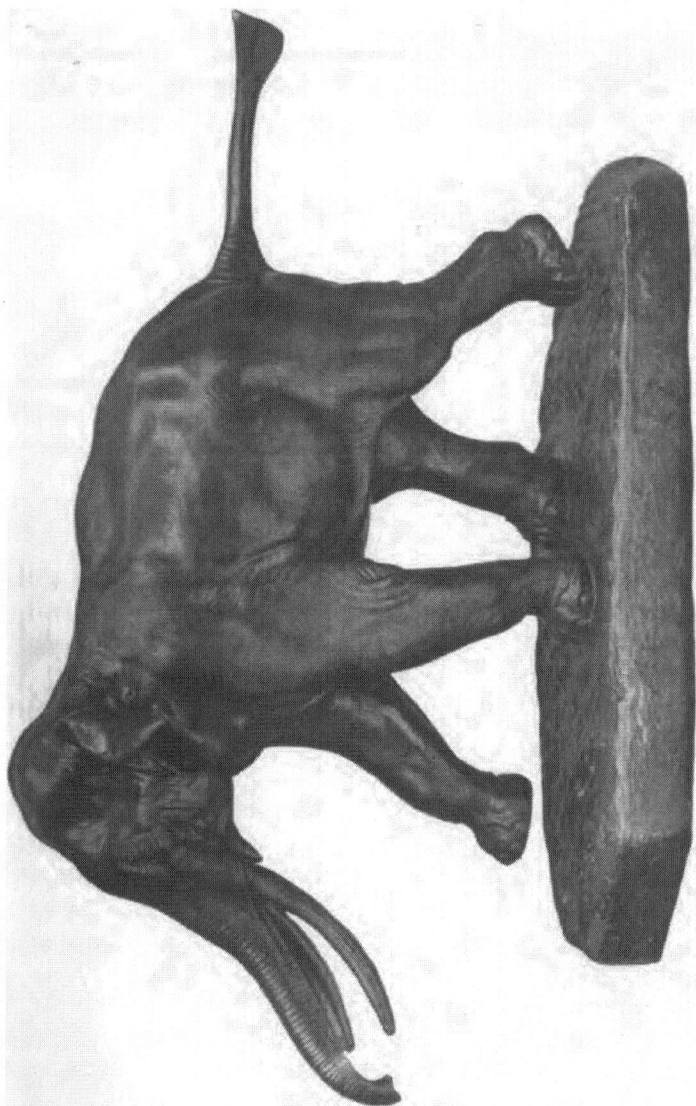

the period, with a comprehensive instinct for grouping, and a skill in fashioning man, domestic animals and wild beasts down to the minutest details, that no artist of any age, of any nation before or since his time has ever surpassed.

Here was a showing that would have almost justified any sculptor in taking from that time forth a position of proud aloofness, an attitude of indifference to criticism. It will be seen that Barye never presumed to hold such a position. He must have known his own genius. But the testimony of Americans who knew him well during the last decades of his life goes to prove that the reserve which was always his characteristic was a natural one, that he was a singularly modest man, and that only on the rarest occasions did he let fall a word which showed he knew — what indeed he could not fail to know — his own genius.

II

THE Salon of 1833 accepted also a frame of medallions and no less than six water colors, which testify how he had employed his time during the years that had failed to bring him into notice. There were careful drawings of Bengal tigers, Cape lions, Peruvian jaguars. There was a tiger devouring a horse, a panther of Morocco and one from India. These had been studied at the Jardin des Plantes, at traveling menageries, or wherever else Barye could learn of great cats in their melancholy confinement.

The Jardin is a delightful spot at a distance from the busiest parts of Paris, whither nurse-maids take the children and families of citizens come to while away the morning of a holiday. At present there is little chance of interruption by friends of the artistic or literary worlds, and in Barye's early days there was far less. Here he would sit on a bench to watch the action of the beasts at feeding time and strive to catch with crayon the movements natural to them, afterwards putting in the color, which with him, unlike Delacroix, was a secondary consideration, so far as the sketches are concerned. Sometimes he pulled from his pocket a lump of wax and made a rough sketch of a head or caught the angry or the amorous curl of a tail.

It was such childish, such antediluvian practises as this that gave to hands drilled by the hard labor with the jewelers and military ornament makers that marvelous rapidity which is needful to seize the movement of animals. It is Barye who has taught us to see the enormous size of the feet of tigers and panthers. They have always been large. But the painters and sculptors of lions and tigers, taking counsel with themselves as to the canons of grace in modern times, have almost always made the extremities small, even smaller than those of the domestic cat, whose feet need not be large because its food consists of little birds and rodents. Barye reminds us that the panther, for instance, has feet of unusual bigness, considering the graceful movements of which it is capable. The Greeks did not lessen the real size of feet and hands either with animals or men. The statuette groups from Ionia show the lion with enormous paws. As a rule men and women in Greek sculpture have feet and hands of a size that moderns dare not suggest.

But Barye was not content with a knowledge of animals from the outside. He attended such lectures on anatomy as he might; when they could be had, he dissected wild beasts that died in captivity. He tried to realize how the great rough processes on the bones of a lion held the enormous muscles fast, and what the result was when the beast used them to lance itself through the air. The fur was studied for its peculiarities. What becomes of its planes, Barye asked himself, when the animal lies curled up in sleep, or stretches itself on awakening, or grapples with its enemies, or stands growling and alert over its quarry? Any cat or dog will be seen to present peculiarities of this sort, but bears, panthers and beasts having abundant fur and skins loosely connected with the flesh often show much stronger changes in the lay and folding of their hides. All these were subjects for Barye to ponder. While doing so we may well imagine those firm lips of his to have settled more and more into the strong lines of concentration that steady thought usually carves about the mouth.

NO. 22.

HORSE SURPRISED BY YOUNG LION

Height 16½ inches

III

THIS year of 1833 is memorable in the life of Barye for one thing more important than any mentioned before. It saw his first commission for a public statue realized. A lion with one great paw clutching a serpent and lips raised from the enormous canine teeth in a growl marked itself out from all the other sculpture of 1832 as fitted for erection the size of life on some square or in some public garden of Paris.

The modeling of the lion was intense with reality, and though the act of destroying another animal much its inferior in strength was not exactly fitted to the character given the king of beasts by the men of the middle ages, yet mankind has such an instinctive antipathy to the snake, Christians, Moslems and Jews are so filled with a hatred of the snake as the symbol of wickedness and betrayal, that the true animality of the lion's action was overlooked by those who might object to realism, were that aspect of the matter presented to their minds. The serpent, lying helpless beneath the wide soft paw for the greater part of its length, doubles back on itself and opens its jaws in hopeless menace. For it is of the python variety that lives in Africa and has no poison fangs wherewith to sell its life for that of its destroyer. The hind feet of the lion are expressive too; in the act of seizing something the saber-like nails on the forefeet flash out to their greatest length from ambush in the folds and long hair of the paw, while those of the hind feet start half-way out in sympathy with the others.

There is a variant on this group reproduced in the artotype in which the left hind leg has caught part of the serpent, while the forefoot, instead of being on the serpent, is lifted high in air at the instant of smiting the reptile, just as a kitten will draw off to strike at its play-mate in sport or in anger. It is a vivid little group, extremely clever in its way, but it does not possess the seriousness, nor the quality of repose which is needed for a large statue. Whether it was a study for the great statue or an after-thought I do not know.

Luckily for Barye and the world the government bought his Lion Crushing the Serpent, those responsible for the purchase thinking to themselves, it may be, that here was a symbolical group in which their party was the lion, the malcontents the serpent. It was lucky, because, although the statue was not placed in any conspicuous spot, but on the contrary in a somewhat secluded corner of the Tuileries, where few people were apt to come, yet it stood where a connoisseur could feel some of its beauty and experience a little of that strange mixture of remorselessness, realism and good taste in art which is found in many of the sculptor's works. The spot was not too complimentary; the group was placed at a height unsuited for examination, being considerably too high for the best view of it; yet at least there was one place in Paris where the great innovator could be seen and after a fashion judged.

Another piece of good luck for Barye was the casting. It was done by a famous bronze-founder named Honoré Gonon whose sons were also skilled in the art, and the process is that called à cire perdue, because the model is wrought in wax and covered with a thick coat of plaster and then subjected to heat. The wax runs off, leaving every delicate line made by the sculptor's boaster exactly reproduced in the mold. Observe in the wood-cut of this group how the hair of mane and tail has been shown in the bronze. Or examine the plaster cast at the Museum in Central Park, New York. If the bronzeman is an expert he will know how to fill every such fine inward dent in the mold with bronze of the best quality, unblemished by air bubbles, and so perfect that the slow and unsatisfactory chiseling of the cast shall not be needed. The process requires great skill and is, or used to be, very expensive. Fortunate was Barye in these points, if in few others.

Life had indeed begun to smile for the young sculptor, already married and a father, but very far from having escaped the ills and ignominies of poverty. After such rebuffs as he had won ten years earlier from the Salon it was a subject for congratulation to have them accept so many groups, figures, water colors and medallions. But to have a group bought

32

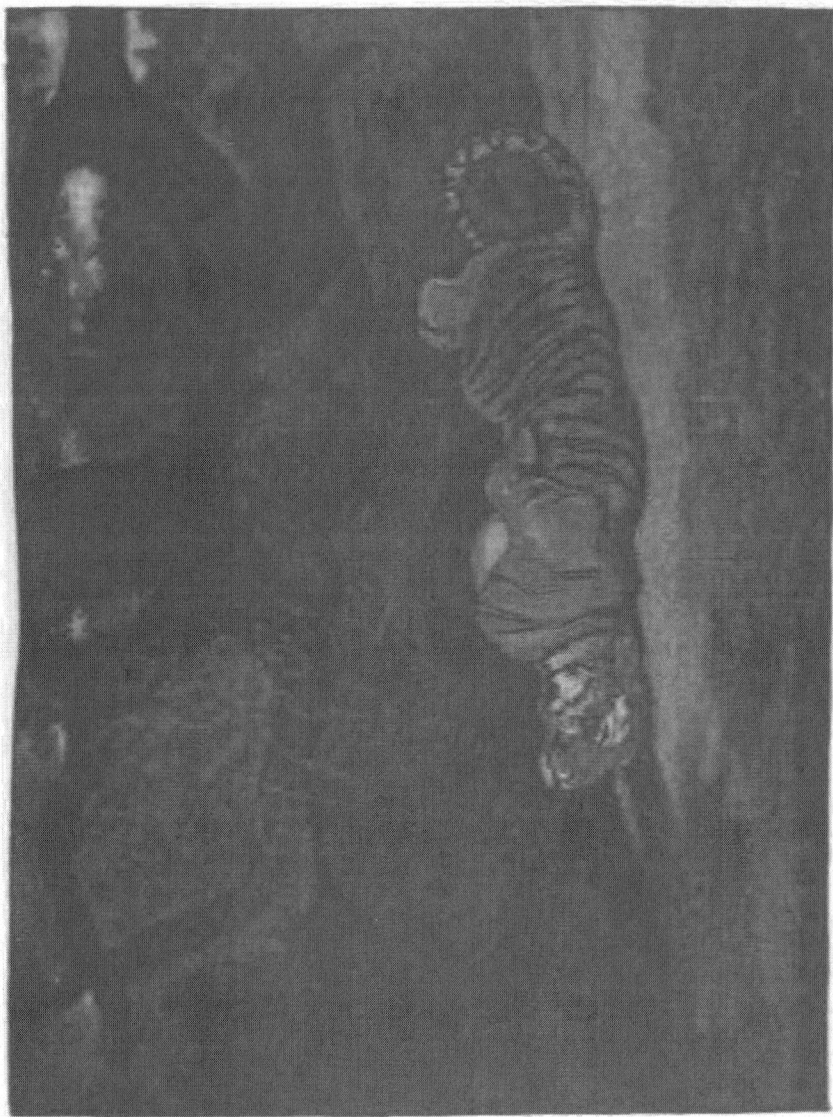

No. 98. TIGER ROLLING (water-color),

10 x 18 inches.

Walters Collection.

by government for a public site was enough to turn his head. Close on the heels of this success came the decoration as Chevalier of the Legion of Honor with the coveted right to wear a small end of red ribbon in the buttonhole, at sight of which the ubiquitous French sentry is bound to present arms. Many other attentions and conveniences are offered to the wearer of the red ribbon. The Prince of the blood was his patron as well as the Princess Marie, for to the Prince Royal went that jovial little statuette the Bear in its Trough, which M. Barbédienne has cast in bronze and popularized in copies that retain a good deal of Barye's power. Patronage in high places was about to cause Barye to undertake some of the most notable groups he ever produced, groups, in the opinion of some critics, which have never been surpassed by their maker but which also gained him enemies for artistic reasons of the base sort and enemies by the way of politics.

Meantime the Lion Crushing the Serpent was duly cast by Gonon and his two sons (1835) and placed in the Tuileries gardens hard by the Avenue des Feuillants where you look down from the terrace upon the hard clean lines of the quays of the Seine. There it has stood while one party after another has arisen to call itself the lion and brand its opposition with the name of serpent. At the Universal Exposition of 1889 in Paris a cast from it was given a very conspicuous place and another has crossed the sea to be treasured as the gift of the French Government to the Metropolitan Museum of New York.

IV

THE angry sneer of a sculptor of the period: 'What! are the Tuileries to become a menagerie?' sets the text for much of the ill-success befalling Barye during the next twenty years. The reasons were many why artists and others who might have been expected to admire were in the ranks of the indifferent or the hostile. The conservatives in art, literature, politics, religion, were in general averse to such a new departure as the elevation of animals to a level with man and the exhibition of their tragedies, apart from man's aid or enmity, in sculpture as serious and materials as rich as those used for the lords of creation.

But it was not only the animal in the Tuileries group that angered some observers, and they the most learned, the professionals, in fact, on whose words even the professed critics of art had to hang with respect. The sculptor who uttered that indignant witticism was most probably willing enough to see the Tuileries peopled with groups of animals on condition that they were modeled according to the canons in art professed by himself, his masters and fellow-workmen. What he really meant was a refusal to accept, not the presence of animal statuary in the Tuileries, but animals fashioned as Barye modeled them. His dislike was for the way in which Barye composed, the method he used for indicating mane and shorter fur. It was a hatred for technical reasons translated into a witticism which could be understood by the laity.

Barye had not modeled the mane and fur of his lion according to rules. There is a look of slovenliness to those trained in other methods about the big flocks of hair which to us seem so admirably expressive of the rude vigor of a lion. But we have learned to accept a broad treatment of sculpture. We have been broken in to the idea by learning to appreciate broad treatment in painting. Modern painters have gone beyond Delacroix in scorn of form and extravagance of coloration. M. Auguste Rodin has gone beyond Barye, Préault and Rude in a suggestive sculpture that employs planes and masses where classicals insist that fair curves and delicate precise outlines should be found. The men of generalizations have carried their banner against the array of particularists and won many a hard fought battle without gaining such a victory as would settle the question forever. We may set against the sneer of the sculptor the remark that Rousseau the landscapist made to his pupil Letronne about this very group of Lion and Serpent:

'The magnificent lion of Barye which is in the Tuileries has all his fur much more truly than if the sculptor had modeled it hair by hair.'

No. 24. LION CRUSHING SERPENT. TUILERIES.
Bronze. Height, 4 feet 2 inches.

Yet this breadth in Barye's work had not come to him easily or at once. We have only to examine the Tiger Attacking a Gavial of the Ganges to perceive that in 1830, when it was wrought out by the sculptor, Barye was still in the toils of the particularists, still wasting much force in unnecessary details which not only wearied the maker but the beholder, if the latter had a true understanding of the aims of art. The ground about the struggling beasts is sown with small trivial objects, vegetable and otherwise, that break it up and extort from the ignorant the pleasure that they feel in laboriousness, but from the wise, pity for a useless expenditure of work. The animals share this trait. They are modeled with anxiety rather than with that easy sweeping power which Barye rose to in the Lion Crushing the Serpent and to still greater power at a later period. The poses are artificial beyond any other group.

I do not wish to imply that the group is not wonderful and admirable in almost every way, but if it have a fault it lies in this excessive attention to detail. Perhaps it was fortunate that Barye did not model them on big planes and with the rush of the impressionist. It is always possible, given a silent man of his known character, that he already knew enough in 1830 to prefer the broader handling, but as a wise man made certain concessions to the inveterate prejudice of his judges and gave them such modeling as they could appreciate. Certainly two years later we find him emancipated. It is also nearly certain that a good many very small objects in bronze that show the same breadth of treatment should be placed during his later 'prentice years with Fauconnier the jeweler.

He was not without advice, however, that the Tiger Attacking the Gavial might have been improved by less anxiety as to details, by the suppression of a lot of unimportant matters which divert and confuse the eye. An anonymous critic in the press who turned out to be Gustave Planche urged the point. The question we have to decide is, whether or not Barye really needed the advice. He seems to have heeded it. But as we have just seen, there is reason to believe that the criticism was less in the nature of a truth revealed than an utterance which emboldened the sculptor to assert what he had already discovered for himself and to some extent put in action.

We may think of Barye at this period as flushed with courage as he stands on the brink of a great career, admired by the strongest men of the young school of landscapists just beginning their work, applauded by the cleverest, most original men of the press, receiving orders from the royal family and great aristocrats—and cordially detested by the old school in art, by the envious and by the devout. In external things Paris is so Latin that we find it a contradiction when we learn that Barye, who was always taciturn, frequented cafés and belonged to what we may loosely call dining clubs composed of friends and comrades somewhat alike in aims. Stories are told of Barye which exhibit him in the light of a bad-tempered and sharp-tongued man; others that give the impression that he hid himself away from his fellowmen and passed a large part of his time in gloomy meditation. They serve well enough to put spice into a hasty composition for the daily press, but they repose on foundations that are lamentably sandy. Indeed one may say that there is almost nothing in them. True is probably the remark attributed to Barye, when questioned as to his invincible silence at the repasts in restaurants which form in France so distinctive a feature in contrast to an unsocial side of American life: 'There are' said he 'two kinds of men, the talkers and the listeners. I belong to the latter.'

That remark, of course by no means original with him, is exactly in accord with his temperament. Like General Grant he did not talk. He detested so much to write a letter that most of his correspondence was carried on by his wife or his daughter. Hence his autograph is rare. His manners to those who came to buy his wares and were sufficiently amateurs to make it worth attending to, were simple, dignified and reserved. But though he generally left his sales to others of the family there was no trace of bad temper about him when he did appear, no sharp speeches, no moodiness, no ungeniality, only a constant sadness. He had learned the lesson of the thousand silences of which Emerson

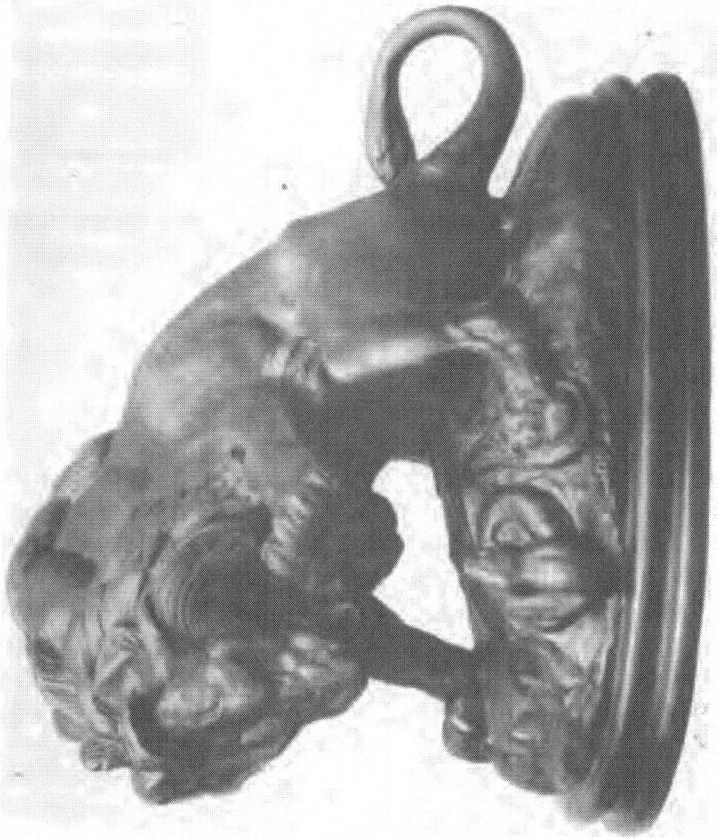

speaks. His were neither boorish silences, nor embittered, nor embarrassed, nor sullen. He loved best to be alone, for it was then that he could reason out best the problems he had set himself to solve.

Yet his nature craved the voices of men; he loved to hear his vivacious friends dispute, without being called on to add his opinion to the debate; and he probably found that his countrymen were for the most part quite ready to welcome a man who accepted so readily the roll of listener. It is said that there is no better means to a reputation for wisdom and amiability than a habit of silence. It is also said that few persons are gifted with the genius of being good listeners. This may account for the fact that Barye, who had a nature perhaps oftener found in Germany and the British Isles than Paris, was loved and cherished by many men of different natures and temperaments, to whom he brought the boon of his ears instead of the embarrassment of a tongue.

V

BARYE'S personality being mooted, there is room here for a matter that may seem at first to contain as much fancy as fact. It will be noticed that in 1831 he modeled the bear in its trough, shown in the artotype, while the Salon of 1833 accepted figures of no less than four bears, namely the Russian, the Alpine, the Indian and the American, the last two in a wrestling match as the wood-cut shows. It may seem to us a simple and even natural thing to use the bear in the fine arts, but that is because this sculptor set the fashion, and clumsy Bruin no longer surprises or disgusts the dilettant. But even in 1830 the animals were ranked by castes.

Ever since the Crusades, when the aristocracy of Europe learned good manners and civilized customs from the Asiatics and Greeks, the lion had been the correct animal for sculpture and the fine arts generally. The horse was allowed a humble position because he belonged to the knight, and the hound came in on sufferance for the same reason. But in the arts horse and hound lost from their servile condition as regards man and were almost always badly drawn or carved, even by the great masters. At the best they were wrought well, but after a set pattern, with small regard to breed and none to individuality. The ox was too much the friend of the rustic; the ass was an object of derision; the serpent was eschewed because paganism still lingered among the pagani or rustics in a thousand superstitions; the boar smacked too much of the ancient heroes before the Crusades who were no longer the fashion; the hare was cowardly and the wolf had almost vanished with increase of population during the comparatively unbloody wars of the middle ages.

In 1830 the bear was not noble any longer, though thousands of names in the various tongues of Europe testified at what a pitch of admiration the ancient Kelts, Teutons and Turanians had once held poor Bruin. Yet the people were true to him long after the middle ages, attributing to his fat restorative powers and to his flesh the property of making the eater courageous. Olaus Magnus of Upsala says that in the northern lands, concerning which he professed to speak with particular authority, the flesh of the bear was cured in large quantities for the use of soldiers. Many are the odd anecdotes he has preserved out of the folk-lore of the middle ages with regard to the bear. Thus the astuteness of Bruin is shown in concealing himself under leaves until deer and cattle approach near enough to be seized, also in his building himself a winter retreat in which to hibernate. The ancients believed that bears grew fat during their winter sleep, and Olaus tells us that it was done by sucking the right paw. This approaches magic.

Human intelligence was accorded the bear in its dealing with the porcupine which it cannot touch when the latter rolls itself up. The bear was believed to resort to a stratagem not unlike the ancient story of the man, his pet bear and the fly. Mounting a small tree near the ball of spines, the bear was said to fell the tree by its own weight exactly across the porcupine and then devour the crushed prey at leisure. But man's belief in the wisdom as well as the strength and courage of the bear rises highest—short of the supernatural—in the story of the Swiss bear

No. 26. AMERICAN AND INDIAN BEARS WRESTLING.
Bronze. Height, 8¼ inches.

that stole a beautiful young girl and made her his wife, their offspring
founding several families which have reached royal and imperial power
in Germany. These strange and extravagant tales, some of which may
have started with the deeds of men named Bear, who lived a robber life
and wore bear's furs for warmth as well as to scare the more peaceful
countrymen, are only mentioned to give some idea of the importance
that once attached in Europe and Asia to a beast now fallen in public
esteem.

For such reasons it was that a sculptor who made bears the subjects
of his works met squarely the caste feeling which had spread from the
ranks of men to animals. Without intending it, he proclaimed himself
thereby a democrat and the champion of the folk, among whom the
bear retained some of his old honor, such as it was. In Reynard the
Fox, a mediæval satire on men by means of beasts, the relative position
of the bear is exactly reflected as it was after the first crusade had introduced the lion generally to Europe. In that delightful chronicle the
bear has aspirations toward the throne and is gulled readily into the
belief that he can take the place of the lion; but his attempts are only
the signal for his utter plunder and bedevilment. Broadly considered
he represents the folk which aims at regaining the command that after
a fashion it once had. The folk hopes to unseat the king, a noble who
has brought the rest of the nobility under his yoke and by their aid
keeps the folk in subjection.

On still wider lines the bear represents the older inhabitants of
Europe, largely composed of Turanians conquered by Aryan tribes.
The lion, an exotic unknown to the fauna of Europe save in Thessaly, at
a remote period, namely at the Persian invasion of Greece, stands for
the conquering race, whose advent into Europe, remote as it is, con-
tinues to be recognized as later than the Turanian. Consciousness of
its past lingers in the present among the commons. We see then how
far rooted back in the past such apparently trivial things are, how
great a history lies behind such a phenomenon as the position of the
bear toward the lion in Reynard the Fox and the bestiaries of the

middle ages. That this is not a fanciful view may be worth proving from the Kalevala of the Finns, an epic which is one of the very few survivals down to the present day of the literature of that Turanian race which once held all Europe from the Urals to the Arran Islands off Ireland and from the North Cape to Sicily, that race which forms a large part of the population of Europe, though its tongues are gone and its legends appropriated by the conquerors.

VI

IN that epic and in the songs of nations of kindred speech which have held their own in the north of Europe there is no talk of the lion. The bear, the wolf, the elk and the reindeer, the horse and the dog, are the nobles, as they used to be elsewhere in Europe. The bear is even more. He ranks there as he did with our Indians who always apologized when they killed him. Bruin is in a certain sense a god to whom are attributed some of the magical properties imagined in the constellation still widely known as the Great Bear. When hunted certain formulas are chanted in his presence before and while he is attacked. The bear hunter's return to the village or farm is accompanied by words consecrated by tradition, solos recited by the killer of the bear, choruses chanted by the villagers, while dances, genuflexions and other signs of a genuine religious rite of a purely pagan character are performed. In the present day a larger element of humor has intruded into these songs but the serious foundation of the ceremonies is abundantly apparent.

Rune XLVI of the Kalevala describes how Vaino, the eponymous hero and benefactor of Finland, undertakes to slay the great bear which Louhi, the traditional enemy of the Finns, has sent down from the northland to devastate the herds and devour the folk of Vainola. He applies to his brother demi-god, the magic smith Ilmarinen, for a weapon capable of piercing the enchanted beast.

No. 27. STANDING BEAR.
Bronze. Height, 9¼ inches.

Thereupon the skillful blacksmith
Forged a spear from magic metals,
Forged a lancet triple-pointed,
Not the longest, nor the shortest,
Forged the spear in wondrous beauty.
On one side a bear was sitting,
Sat a wolf upon the other,
On the blade an elk lay sleeping,
On the shaft a colt was running,
Near the hilt a roebuck bounding.

Here are the old noble animals of Europe before ideas of kingship and a graded aristocracy were fixed, at first by Charlemagne and then more firmly by the upper classes during the Crusades — bear, wolf, elk, horse and stag. The bear leads them all.

Vaino then addresses the rulers of the forest, asking their permission and aid and begging them to chain up their 'dogs' the wolves. He proceeds to invoke Otso the bear, calling him forest-apple, honey-paw, light-foot, well-beloved and other terms of admiration and endearment, charming him in such fashion to acquiesce in his own death. That stern fact is clothed in all sorts of circumlocutions. Otso is promised fine quarters, milk, honey and a magnificent entertainment in Vainola. When they hear the strain of Vaino's bugle on the hills the people rush from their cabins and ask a series of questions in which the feelings of the bear are most delicately considered. And Vaino answers:

Therefore do I come rejoicing,
Singing, playing, on my snow-shoes.
Not the mountain-lynx nor serpent,
Comes however to our dwelling;
The Illustrious is coming,
Pride and beauty of the forest;
'Tis the Master comes among us,
Covered with his friendly fur-robe.
Welcome Otso, welcome Light-foot,
Welcome Loved one from the glenwood!
If the mountain guest is welcome,
Open wide the gates of entry;
If the bear is thought unworthy,
Bar the doors against the stranger.

There are formulas when the bear is skinned and his flesh prepared for the cauldrons. And while all who are worthy partake of the sacred banquet Vaino is questioned concerning Otso's birth and deeds; whereupon he answers in a very beautiful, nay, a lovely panegyrie, in which the connection between the physical bear and the spiritual god of the constellation is everywhere apparent. He pushes civility so far as to assert that the dead bear was not brutally killed by him, but out of regard for the people actually committed suicide by falling from a tree and impaling himself on a stake. As to Otso's birth, that was celestial so far as his soul is concerned; he was fashioned by the daughter of the god of the woodlands out of materials thrown from heaven into the sea by a maiden of the sky, and was cradled in the top of a pine.

Fair Mielikki, woodland hostess,
Tapio's most cunning daughter,
Took the fragments from the seaside,
Took the white wool from the waters,
Sewed the hair and wool together,
Laid the bundle in her basket,
Basket made from bark of birch-wood,
Bound with cords the magic bundle;
With the chains of gold she bound it
To the pine-tree's topmost branches.
There she rocked the thing of magic,
Rocked to life the tender baby
'Mid the blossoms of the pine-tree
On the fir-top set with needles;
Thus the young bear well was nurtured,
Thus was sacred Otso cradled
On the honey-tree of Northland
In the middle of the forest.

Sacred Otso grew and flourished,
Quickly grew with graceful movements,
Short of feet, with crooked ankles,
Wide of mouth and broad of forehead,
Short his nose, his fur-robe velvet.
. . . . . .
Then she freed her new-made creature,
Let the Light-foot walk and wander,

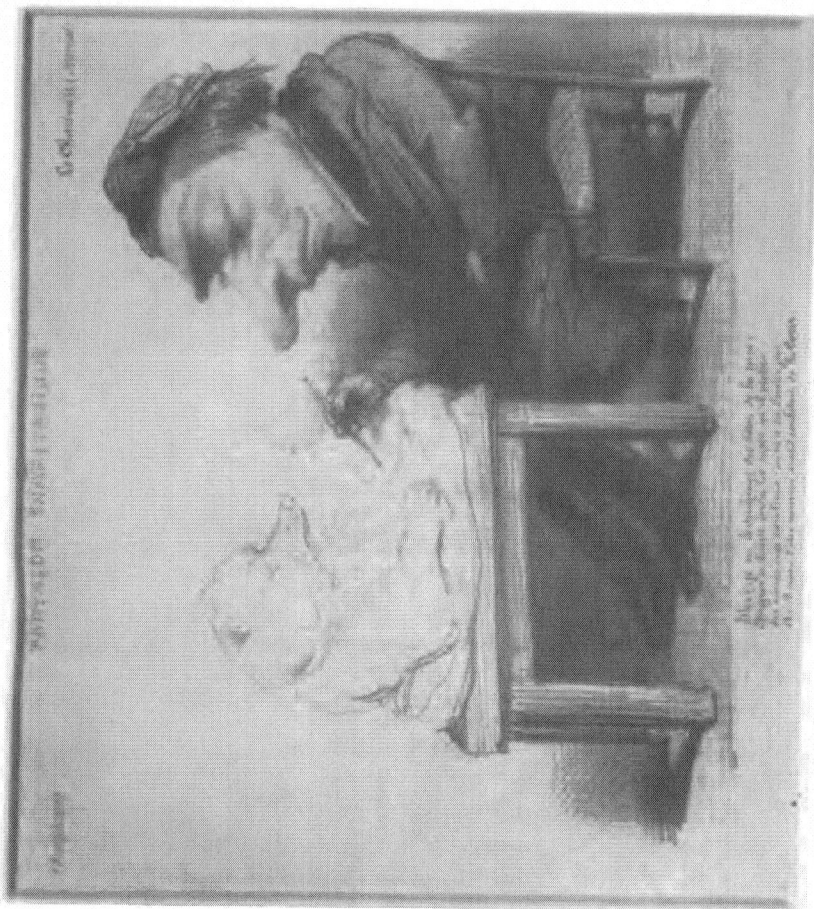

NO. 28.

BARYE CARICATURED AS A BEAR

Let him lumber through the marshes,
Let him amble through the forest,
Roll upon the plains and pastures;
Taught him how to walk a hero,
How to move with graceful motion,
How to live in ease and pleasure,
How to rest in full contentment
In the moors and in the marshes
On the borders of the woodlands.

(J. M. Crawford's Kalevala.)

The meaning of Otso's double birth in heaven and on earth is discovered when we perceive that the magic bear, sent by Louhi the spirit of the northern storm to devastate Finland, is an earthly double of Otava the Great Bear of the heavens, who is considered more particularly a god of the Lapps and the northern Finnic peoples but little touched by Christianity.

VII

THE stag and the lion were the noble animals in particular when Barye startlèd Paris with his bears single and bears double. Undoubtedly there is a comic element in the bear well understood by the hardy peasants of the Béarnais who capture and train the common brown bear to dance for the delectation of children and rustics. But in French, Belgian and English heraldry the favorite animal is the lion, showing as before noted the strong influence exerted by the Crusades. For who, looking over a manual of heraldry, would imagine that the beast that meets the eye at every turn has no existence in Europe save in the guise of a wretched captive at fairs and in menageries? And why is it that one sees so rarely the bear, which once was the synonym of courage and strength?

Because the upper classes turned naturally to exotic symbols in order to widen yet more the gulf between them and the common herd. Scottish and German ballads and chronicles have many variants on the old travelers' tales setting forth how a hero from Europe, journeying through Oriental lands, despatches a very large cat, as he supposes, and finds that he has slain the monarch of beasts, so much dreaded by the natives. Doubtless such things did occur. A Crusader clad in steel may have killed a lion or a leopard in Palestine or Egypt. But the fashion was set to place one of these beasts on the shield and, later, in the quarterings of coats-of-arms, in order to publish the claim of the wearer to descent from a soldier who fought for the Cross in the East or perchance to boast that the ancestor in question slew a valiant Saracen whose shield carried a lion as a blason. It seems odd that such a thing should have its effect down to the present day; but so it is.

We know that Barye surprised the men of 1830 by his bears more than anything else, because, when a caricaturist of a sort by no means ill-natured wished to make sport of the sculptor as of other artists, he drew Barye seated at his modeling table in the act of molding the statuette of a bear. The illustration shows this lithograph, which must be regarded as a witness to Barye's fame rather than an attack upon him. The verses below it are very poor, but they have no sting. The object was simply to provoke a smile and doubtless did so merely from the fact that the bear itself was generally regarded an un-noble animal hardly suited to the fine arts. But what must strike one further is the fact that the caricaturist has found in Barye's face a likeness to that of Bruin. By exaggerating enormously the generous nose with its rising plane below the tip wherewith the sculptor was blessed, the fun-maker has managed to bring the profiles of man and beast into some kind of resemblance. We may doubt whether to anybody else this comparison occurred. But there is a coincidence connected with it that is of course nothing more than a coincidence, yet perhaps worthy of note. It relates to the probable origin of the sculptor's family name.

The bear having once stood at the head of all the animals of Europe for strength and courage, was a favorite for the names of boys. Thence it entered into a great series of names, not of men alone, but of districts and lands. Berne in Switzerland carries the bear on its coat-of-arms. Béarne in the south of France, Beara in the southwest of Ireland

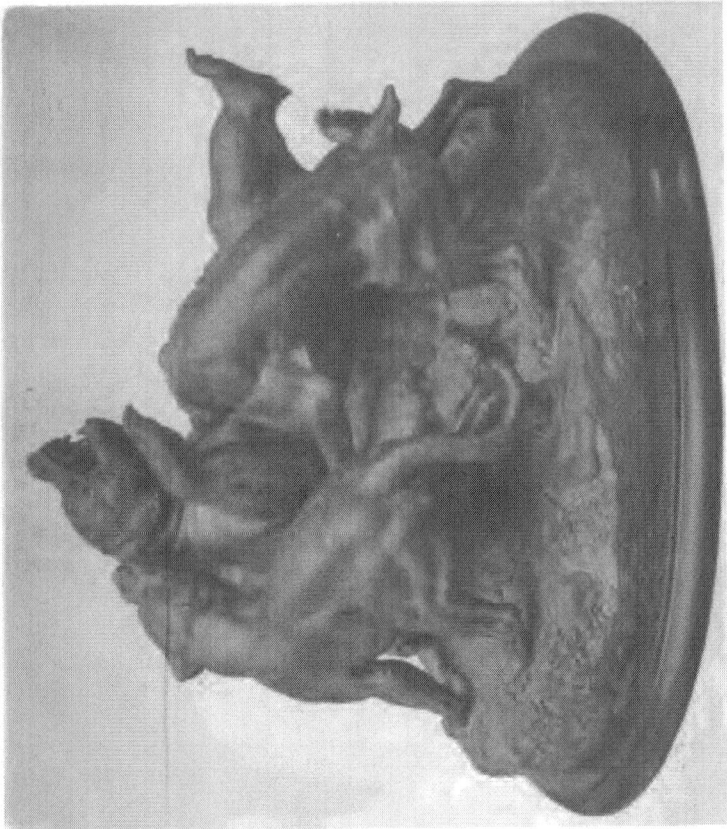

named from a mythical princess from Spain, Biarma-land near the Arctic sea are places in point. Berlin and Prussia (Borussia) belong to the bear. The title of Baron may be traced by various steps to the strong man in general who for his valor and strength was called a bear. There is more than a probability that the name Barye is one of a host of such names. These may be profitably compared with a great number of names in the present day into which the word lion or leon, Löwe or Leuw enters, according as the family descends from French, English, Italian, German or Hollandish stock. The place-names into which bear enters may likewise be compared with place-names in which lion is found. And it may be further remarked that as a rule the bear names belong to an older period than the lion names; also that the lion names are apt to be borne by those of the upper classes or by such people as have assumed upper-class names in order to separate themselves from common folk.

Bear names for individuals are found in almost all languages, but our composite tongues of Europe generally favor two forms. One, the northern, seems to spring from the old non-Aryan languages of Europe and is represented by *piro, bero* in Finnish, *Bär* in German, *björn* in Norwegian, *bear* in English. The other, the southern, is found as *aksha* in Sanskrit, *arktos* in Greek, *ursus* in Latin, *ours* in French. The modern word for bear in Finnish is *karhu* meaning the 'rough, hairy' animal but the old word for a beast that is still worshipped by remote sections of the Turanian races in Asia is preserved by the Finns in *Piru*, devil. In Lappish we have *biran*, the bear, while in the dialects spoken by the Koibals and Karagasses the word has been applied to the wolf, which is more dangerous on the steppes than the forest-dwelling bear. *Bür* and *bürü* are their terms for the wolf. Fitz-Urse is a name the Normans brought into England. Björn is an appellation one meets constantly in the Norse sagas; indeed there is one tale of a prince of that name who was bewitched by a woman called Bera (she-bear) who caused him to marry her, but soon occasioned the death of her husband and his brother Ingvé at each other's hands. The famous hero of the Saxon lay of Béowulf is called Bee-wolf, a word that means no other animal than the bear. In the well-known mediæval tale on the other hand there is Orson, the boy who was brought up by the bears; Ursula 'little she-bear' is a name not unknown to the Latins before and after Christian times. We may confidently place then the majority of names like Barry and Barye in the great class deriving from powerful animals and rank them more particularly under the bears.

Barye was in every sense a man of the people, a common soldier in the wars, an apprentice to a jeweler, defective in his education, unpretentious, a member of that vast body of men in France who let others do the talking and posturing but keep the country upright, sound in morals and teeming with wealth. He was it is true patronized by a king, by princes and princesses of the blood royal, by Bourbons and Napoleons; but the instinct of the man revealing itself in his daily life—his sober industrious habits, his excellent record as husband, father and citizen—was for democracy. The aim of the sculptor, revealing itself in the new field of work into which he entered with calm confidence in his own wisdom against the fashion and indeed the clamorous opposition of his day, was toward a subtler democracy in the arts. A better example of this fact could not be wished than the appearance in the Salon of 1833 and succeeding exhibitions of all those statuettes of the bear, that animal which the history of Europe for the past eight hundred years had consigned to unmerited contempt, while the beast of the court and camp, the favorite of the nobility, the animal after which towns, villages, nobles hastened to call themselves was not only foreign to the soil but the symbol of an upper class more inimical to the people, more destructive of wealth and comfort than would have been a legion of bears.

Barye, the descendant of some conqueror of bears into whose name that mark of steady courage was stamped, in whose profile a caricaturist even detected a likeness to that of a bear, surprised the world by deigning to employ his acknowledged talent as a sculptor in modeling a thoroughly unfashionable, an almost ridiculous beast.

46

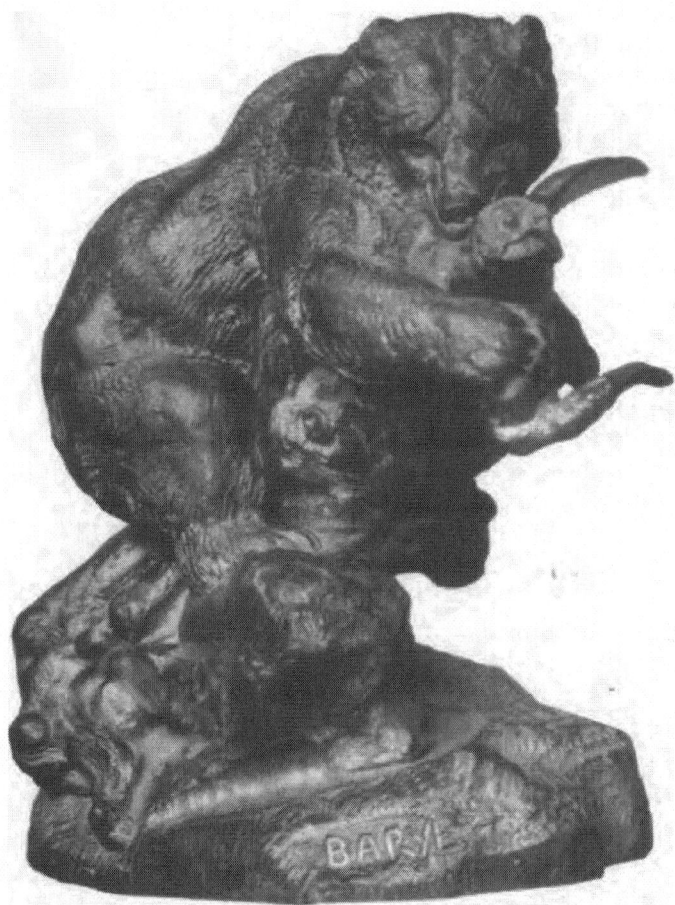

NO. 31.

BEAR SURPRISING OWL

Height 7¼ inches

VIII

UNDER the encouragement of his successes in 1831 and 1833 the genius of Barye put forth branches in all directions. He was almost too prolific, as we shall see in the next chapter. The little bear rollicking in his tub, which was bought by the heir apparent to the throne, showed at least this to such as were too fashionable to admire that beast: the sculptor could touch the comic string as well as the tragic. He was not an abnormal artist, a lover of carnage and blood, though such is the charge reiterated against him. He could be genial in clay and raise a smile—yet also chill the beholder with the ferocity of beast natures engaged in the last agony of exertion to escape death. The standing bear, too, has a waggish look, and from behind presents the clumsy cumbrous appearance which the unknown bards who transmitted the Kalevala to us have touched upon so finely in the chants to honor Otso the Illustrious One, Forest-apple and Light-foot! What a tender note in his little statuette of a dead gazelle!—there again we see how narrow is the view that perceives in Barye only the cruelty of combat.

We have noted many reasons for opposition to Barye's work that were independent of jealousies of the guild, being naturally the product of ancient ideas partly religious, partly sociological, partly connected with false axioms in art. But now we open the chapter of animosities arising from the success of the sculptor, such as it was; animosities which have been treated by essayists and biographers as if they were the only stumbling-blocks in his way, as if they sprang from pure malignity untempered by reason. We may be certain that up to 1834 the opposition Barye found was unconscious opposition, having no individual bearing and simply resulting from the situation, the inveterate prejudices, the fashionable ideas of the time. With the Salon of 1833 we reach the moment when Barye was a marked man, no longer an unknown or a merely clever artisan who had made a point by chance in a former Salon. With other artists he contributed a cut to Le Musée, revue du Salon de

1834. He was lauded by men like Gustave Planche, Thoré, Théophile Gautier, Silvestre. But these writers were prone to attack the men in office as their successors are to-day; whilst those in office, together with the writers and artists who hoped for favors, answered them in the public prints, or more often, having the power in their own hands, affected to ignore the assaults but riposted by withholding awards and honors, and even by refusing to accept and exhibit the work of artists admired by the opposition.

Thus the latter became the victims of a polemic which was all the more poisonous and without ruth because it revolved on matters of taste and dealt with abstractions which are removed from ordinary tests. If you say that a tree is so many feet high, your statement can be verified by actual measurement or by calculations with the aid of an instrument everybody accepts. But if you say that the moon seems to you the size of a quart measure, it is quite within possibilities that one person will say it is the size of the head of a barrel and another that it is as large as a silver dollar. There is no appeal from these differences of opinion because there is no way of measuring the apparent breadth of the moon unless some convention be established, such as the distance from the eye of some unit of measure by which its size can be calculated. The man who admired the bears of Barye and he who regarded bears as too vulgar and ridiculous for sculpture were not likely to convince each other. Still harder to conciliate was the artist who thought Barye slurred his work when he made it broad. But the most irreconcilable were those who were filled with the demon of politics and decided for and against a man according as their leaders gave the signal. It was from these gentry that Barye was now to suffer far-reaching harm.

NO. 32.

ELK SURPRISED BY A LYNX.

Height 8½ inches.

CHAPTER THREE

I

HE Duke of Orleans followed up the favors already granted to Barye by ordering a series of groups to occupy the centre, corners and sides of the middle space on his dining table upon an immense tray of silver, designed by Chenavard, called a *surtout*. The largest was of course for the centre. At the sides groups only less elaborate were to stand, while the corners of the centre-piece were to be graced by four still smaller pieces. Nine groups, the largest of which contained three animals and three men, the smallest, two animals, were to be finished in time for the Salon of 1834. They exist to-day as a proof of the tremendous power of work in Barye during those years of uncertain and then apparently assured success. The centre-piece is the Hunt of the Tiger. Hindoos and Mohammedan Indians on the back of an immense elephant defend themselves against two tigers, one of which clambers up the side of the great brute and almost reaches the howdah on its back, while the other has fastened its fangs and claws in the left hind foot of the elephant.

This truly superb bronze, which deserved to be made life-size and placed as a memorial of Barye in the Jardin des Plantes where he studied to such purpose, was cast like the lion and serpent of the Tuileries by the wax process. Carved on its base one reads: *Bronze d'un jet sans ciselure. Fondu à l'Hôtel Dangivilliers par Honoré Gonon.* Frightful is the aspect of the tiger that seizes the elephant's leg. Serpentine and beautiful is the other, writhing up the elephant's side. Tremendous is the action of the men; stolid but resolved is the huge beast, round which the fight rages as round a living island conscious of the acts of the pigmies that assail and defend it. Contemplating this piece one is tempted to say that it alone might suffice to give an artist fame and that, had Barye never done but this one group, he would have been almost as famous as he afterwards became. For in great fecundity of invention there is this. As one nail drives out another, so the new work of art causes men to forget the old. The multiplicity of Barye's groups made the public value less the beauty of each.

At one of the ends of the table stood the Hunt of the Elk. Tatars on horseback pursue the noble quarry, and having overtaken two elks with their dogs, are just in the act of driving at the throat of one with hanger and spear. On one side rose the Hunt of the Wild Ox, a beast now almost extinct in Europe and one which has not been a wild animal in the usual sense for centuries. Two warriors of the fifteenth century in the simple sort of helmets and breast-plates of Francis I pursue the wild bull, which has already got the better of several big mastiffs. The horses of two hunters have been driven fairly upon the bull so that their forefeet are on its back while a third horseman is fairly under it, his horse having fallen dead. The piece is rather long, not being concentrated into a compact group like the end pieces. The third is the Hunt of the Lion and the fourth the Hunt of the Bear, a singularly well-knit composition, full of rush on the part of the huntsmen and of angry ineffectual fight on the side of the bears. The group is so good that for many critics it surpasses even the tiger-hunt with elephant, the point being that Barye loved bears and rendered them with singular spirit, and furthermore that a bear hunt is a scene not unknown in Europe, while a tiger-hunt requires in a European artist a good deal of imagina-

No. 34. HUNT OF THE TIGER.
Bronze. Height, 27 inches.

tion to take the place of study from the life. There are two bears and
several dogs; one huntsman on horseback, of the time of Charles VII,
is about giving with a sword a splendid right cut from the left side of
his head; another on foot has closed with a bear. For many reasons this
group may well be ranked first among the four pieces at ends and sides;
but a careful examination of the groups now in the Walters Gallery must
lead to the conclusion that the centre-piece, the Tiger-hunt, is the most
imposing if not the closest to reality. The Walters Gallery lacks but
one of this famous quintette. The Lion-hunt has not left France. The
Bear-hunt was formerly in the collection of the late William Tilden
Blodgett of New York.

The varied shapes of the nine groups are only understood when their
relative positions are considered. Imagine an enormous baronial table
bearing a *surtout* laid with mirrors and lit by brilliant masses of tapers.
Then the Tiger-hunt occupied the centre. On the long sides of the
table stood the Lion-hunt and Wild-bull-hunt forming long rather than
round masses of combatants. Toward the ends on elevated parts
of the tray were the Elk-hunt and Bear-hunt, rounded in general
outline. Finally the four duels of animals were to stand on pedestals
placed at the four corners of the Tiger-hunt in the centre. The arrangement was thus to be symmetrical but not too regular. One
who could appreciate the novelty of the groups and understand all
the learning intimately fused with genius that was needful to have
produced them might well lose his appetite in regarding such master
craft.

Down to 1850 the arbiters of the Salon were the members of the Institute from whose ranks a jury was formed to pass upon the pieces
submitted. Some were booky men who had lived so retired and were
so little dreaded by their peers that they were readily elected to a
House at whose portals a man of brains, active life and enemies knocked
in vain. Others were musicians for whose ability to judge works of art
certain critics expressed deep contempt. These were the men who had
formerly driven Barye to despair and kept him from the Salon. He

had brief favors in 1831 and 1833. Now it came to something more than Barye alone; it was Barye plus the Prince Royal.

It will hardly be believed that such works of art as these were refused by the Salon in the year 1834. The Duke of Orleans had seen them growing beneath the hand of the master and very naturally desired to see them exhibited. He asked the sculptor to see that they might appear, but Barye, either because he felt that he was already marked for a victim of jealousy, or because he was deeply wounded by the taunts of *animalier* and maker of paper-weights and mantel ornaments, or because he felt it to be undignified to exert influence on the jury, declined to act. Thereupon the Duke made overtures and was surprised to find, the groups for the *surtout de table* were to be refused admittance! He hurried to Louis Philippe the head of the State, and begged that such an act of injustice might not be committed. But that monarch had all he could do to maintain himself among difficulties far more important than ebullitions of ill-will among artists and the officials who preside over artistic matters.

'What would you?' remarked Louis Philippe, the upholder on democratic principles of a throne which could only be based on the divine right of kings. 'I have created a jury. I can not force them to accept works of genius.'

Nothing could have placed in a stronger light the insecurity of a throne which really at the last resort rested on the bayonets of a Europe revolted and thrown back, as Europe then was, on the old crude government by kings, through the excesses of the Revolution and the insatiable ambition of Napoleon the Great. The sculptor in question was a revolutionist in art, a man of the people, and the jury was far from being a knot of men who professed democratic sentiments or felt them. Yet the combination of artists who detested any new ideas and of officials who enjoyed the opportunity of snubbing a Duke of Orleans was too strong to be overcome.

There was less excuse for the rejection of these groups owing to the fact that they were each unique, not at all pieces that could offer them-

NO. 35.

HUNT OF THE ELK

Height 20 inches

selves to the objection of being bronzes which might be repeated and
put into commerce as an article of trade. The Duke was a popular man
with the Parisians; the king, his father, showed on several occasions
a decided sensitiveness to the contrast between public expressions of
approval of himself and the heir. It may be that some of the animus
that showed itself against these special groups sprang from the spaniel
trait of courtiers to detect the hidden feelings of their masters and
molest those toward whom the latter cherish ill-will. The death of the
luckless Duke by being thrown from his carriage in the street removed
a courageous and keen-sighted patron of the arts.

When their rejection was assured, the landscapist Jules Dupré, the
last to survive of that glorious band which numbered among them
Millet, Rousseau and Corot, happened to meet Barye as he walked pen-
sive and as usual alone.

He asked the sculptor how things went with him.

'Very well indeed,' answered Barye, 'they have refused my groups
for the Duke of Orleans.'

And when Dupré expressed his surprise and disgust the other
remarked:

'Why, it is easy enough to understand. I have too many friends on
the jury.'

M. Arsène Alexandre is only too right, while telling this anecdote, to
make it a peg on which to hang a sermon upon the cruelty of artists
toward their fellows, a truth less clearly understood in 1833 than it is
at present, when there are so many proofs, to put it mildly, of the
bad judgment of artists in positions of responsibility with regard to
work by their fellow-craftsmen. Yet even here we must always remember that opposition which seems to outsiders the direct product of
professional jealousy is very often honest. It springs from ignorance in
men who have devoted themselves too strictly to one view and one side
of art; who have in youth attached themselves so violently and without
reserve to the ideas of one master, that they occupy the position once
held by the grammarians, who could see nothing beyond their own

laborious horizons and were by their very learning rendered incapable of appreciating and even tolerating a new vista in wisdom.

It is tenable that Barye did not reach his highest point in these five groups. There is an excess of composition and movement in some of them; there is composition in the Wild Bull Hunt for instance which lends itself to criticism when the bronze is regarded by itself. One may say that the dogs and one of the horsemen are a detriment to the group, which would be better understood at a glance were they absent. But one has only to look at the illustration to note what a magnificent outline that composition takes. It must always be remembered that no one of the present generation has seen these superb ornaments of a dinner table all together and placed exactly as the designer intended they should be. Effects which seem purposeless when a group is regarded for itself, and especially [as one falls into the habit of imagining with works by Barye] as it might look if enlarged to colossal proportions or the size of life and placed alone on a public square, may explain themselves when once the whole service has been brought together and made the decoration of a magnificent table glittering with wax candles and relieved by flat mirrors and silver.

The four minor pieces which, as just stated, were the flankers for the Tiger-hunt, consist each of combats between two animals. An eagle pursues a bouquetin, striving to blind it or hurry it from a precipice to its death. A lion seizes a boar and the combat is by no means certainly in favor of the lion. A leopard springs upon an antelope. A serpent has twined itself about a bison or a gnu and tries to crush it. There is some uncertainty as to the whereabouts of these four pieces. It is possible that the Python Crushing a Gnu owned by M. Léon Bonnat the painter, which was recently shown in the Gazette des Beaux Arts under the mistaken title Aurochs and Serpent, is the fourth piece. It is unique and appears to have been made like all this set by the wax process in which the mold is destroyed.

In 1853 when the Duchess of Orleans sold the table service the Eagle and Bouquetin went to London while the other pieces were scattered

NO. 36.

HUNT OF THE BEAR

Height 18 inches

among French amateurs. But four of the groups in chief are now here. A strange and moving decoration, truly, this ninefold drama of the struggle of animals against man and their natural enemies of the plain and forest! The ordinary diner-out of the present day might find such groups decidedly too strong meat for his digestion, although we owe it to the march of science that few now reject the thought that all animate nature is engaged in a ceaseless struggle for life; people of education have become familiar with the harshest facts of the case. But imagine the effect upon the men of 1833 who for the most part were still beneath the spell of Jean Jacques Rousseau and his idyllic views of existence in the woods and pastures! Like some baleful necromancer a plain artisan conjures up in most enduring bronze a spectre of that ferocious by-play of the jungle, the prairie, the old forests of Europe and the frozen morasses of Siberia which is forgot while we clothe ourselves with the spoils of the chase and relate anecdotes of the big game knocked over by the modern arms of precision.

The earnestness of Barye was uncongenial to much that is uppermost in French character and French ideals of taste and good breeding. These astounding groups were shaped not at all for a museum of natural history or the gallery of a rich globe-trotter, where they might form part of his strange bronzes from Japan and his other curiosities, but—of all other places—for the festal board of a prince, and that prince the Bourbon who might some day become the King of France! It was too much for the gay nation, or the nation that tries philosophically to be gay. Verily, in attempting to vie with the makers of *articles de Paris* this man Barye showed the strength, but in one sense also the rude, downright vigor of the bear. But the jury that refused them did not formulate their objections on that line of defense. On the contrary, their defense was that the groups were not sufficiently 'finished'; then they went on to prove too much and convicted themselves of ignorance or of insincerity by saying that these were not sculpture but jeweler's work.

II

THE Salon of 1834 did not, however, reject other sendings by Barye, nor exclude at least one bronze he had made a few years earlier for the Duke of Orleans. This was the little bear already mentioned sporting in his tub; it was cast by the wax process also. Then there was the elephant modeled and cast for the Duke of Nemours and a horse in combat with a lion ordered by the Duke of Luynes. There was a bronze bear and the dead gazelle, now making its appearance in bronze, each a separate piece. He also sent some water-colors, but the number and importance of his contributions were much diminished owing to the rejection of his masterpieces for the Duke's table. A panther throttling a gazelle and a stag surprised by a lynx (plaster) represented the more ferocious side of animal existence as Barye saw it from the singular vantage ground of a dusty workshop in over-civilized Paris. The Stag and Lynx were put in bronze by the wax process for the Duke of Orleans and in 1836 presented by him to Alexandre Dumas the Elder.

The disfavor of the jury was a hard blow, but doubtless Barye was still of good heart and looked confidently to the future, now that he had not only the strongest writers on his side, but an imposing list of patrons in his books. Yet to the Salon of 1835 he sent only a Tiger Devouring a Stag which was executed of colossal size in Charence stone and placed at Lyons, the birthplace of his father. The material cuts easily but hardens with time. This subject he also cast in bronze by the wax process, but of comparatively small size, for Monsieur Thiers who was already collecting the works of art for which his home in Paris became famous. The same or another bronze reduction Barye used to sell for one hundred and twenty francs. Barye perhaps showed in this solitary offering to the Salon his resentment for the act of the jury in 1834. In this year falls the Lion Holding a Guiba Antelope of which the Walters Gallery possesses a specimen covered by a most beautiful golden bronze patina. It has an extra stamp reading 'Barye 17' evidently

added after the casting with a steel punch. Many bronzes by Barye
carry such numbers punched on or underneath their metal stands.

They gave rise to a little legend—for this sculptor had very early
the honor of engendering legends with respect to himself and his
works. They were punched, so the story went, in order to assure Barye
of their identity under distressing circumstances. Forced by poverty
to put them in pawn, he feared that the broker might substitute a copy
for the genuine piece and took this method to authenticate his own
work and make it easy to detect a fraud. Though not destitute of a
certain foundation, the legend as it stands is apocryphal. The meaning of these punched numbers is simply this: Barye was a very scrupulous man who pushed conscientiousness to lengths that gave him no
little financial harm at the time. He did not wish that he should forget,
or any buyer be in doubt, how many copies of a given bronze had been
uttered previous to the one then sold. Stamp 17 in this case meant
that sixteen copies of the Lion and Guiba Antelope had previously been
made. In the end he found numbering copies impracticable and gave it up.
Very few pieces are stamped above one hundred. As regards the patina
however the number did not hold. None of the sixteen might approach
the seventeenth in the beauty of the patina which his skillful care had
spread over the bronze.

For Barye was without a question the most accomplished bronze
founder in the world. Like the Japanese artists, like those of Florence
in the time of Benvenuto Cellini, he was equipped at all points, though
from lack of capital his workshop was not so well appointed as it
might have been. He was not only a master of form; he was a colorist. The secret of the green patinas found on bronzes at Pompeii was
pondered by him. Whether that green was due merely to the mois-
ture of the earth or was also partly due to coloring produced at the
moment of casting, the fact remained that a certain degree of it is
most charming to the eye. A fine color is that on a Walking Elephant
shown in the illustration which belongs to Mr. T. B. Clarke, a light
brown patina. Others are almost black, so dark is the brown or green. .

Barye understood well enough how to give to bronze an even patina that looks like the green varnish we find on lizards in metal from Italy. But he aspired to produce something finer. He wished to catch the effect of a patina of a green tint which lingers in the crevices of a bronze and by handling has been rubbed from the superior planes. Night and day he reflected on methods to enrich bronzes without making them inartistically bright; many were his failures but also signal were his triumphs. In any large collection of his bronzes it is only necessary to observe the variety of greens, bronze-browns and golden-bronzes that meet the eye to assure oneself of his quality as a colorist of a sober but subtle kind. Some of them give the effect of a very close velvet. Others seem like a rich brown bronze in which spicules of gold are embedded. Upon still others a green patina is detected only here and there, but in a general view its effect is produced without being at first accounted for. A great gathering of works by Barye, such as took place this year in the spring at Paris and the autumn at New York, is valuable among other things for the chance it affords to compare the same piece in its different shades and varieties of patina. It is a study which Barye himself did but initiate; circumstances prevented him from carrying it very far.

There is however in this direction a field for the development of bronze surfaces which the founders in Paris like M. Barbédienne have by no means explored. Color in bronze statues has been generally left to chance. When a public statue is cleaned it is scraped and rubbed from top to bottom and a coating applied, the results from which are, that for a time the bronze looks uncomfortably shiny, then grows dull and ends by appearing soiled and covered with streaks and blotches. Study of smaller bronzes will teach the lesson that public monuments should not be overhauled at the end of ten years or so by irresponsible and ignorant employees of some department of a city's government. They should be under the constant care of men who know how by judicious rubbings to bring out the finest points of a bronze and keep these always prominent. It would have been well had Barye put on record what are the

NO. 38.

PANTHER DEVOURING GAZELLE

Height 5¼ inches

best methods of preserving bronze statues, for no one has lived who understood so much on the subject from direct practical research. Moreover he was able to observe for forty-two years the effects of a city atmosphere on one large bronze, the Tuileries lion. Unfortunately he incurred by such studies the ill-will of the professional founders in bronze, who succeeded in giving currency to the report that his green patinas were deleterious to the health of those who cast and owned them.

III

THE patronage of Louis Philippe and his little prime minister did not stop at orders for small bronzes. It considered the employment of such extraordinary talents as Barye had developed for the adornment of the public squares. In his enthusiasm for Barye there was talk by M. Thiers of large figures to decorate the Place de la Concorde, perhaps the most important square of the city. But there were detractors whispering in his ear, or the enthusiasm was but flash in the pan; certain it is that instead of decorating the Place the bridge was proposed, namely the four corners of the parapet on two sides of the Seine. Then the proposition fell to a group for one of the four corners; but there is no evidence that Barye ever got a commission even for that.

Then there was another scheme devised by M. Thiers to afford Barye a chance to show his genius on a grandiose scale. To Rude had been given the decoration of one façade of the Arc de Triomphe, to sculptors of high rank but commonplace works the other reliefs. The little states-man felt that Barye was the man to put the finishing touch to the Arc de Triomphe by a piece of sculpture in which prettiness and 'finished' workmanship had no part, something grand and simple which might gather up into itself the superb idea of the armies of the republic sallying forth and subjugating the kings of the rest of Europe.

Barye was asked to submit a design. Barye submitted the design. It was a large model of an Eagle, about seventy feet from tip to tip of its outspread wings, alighting on the spoils of war gathered from many nations. This should symbolize the Grand Army on the top' of the newly finished arch. It should also symbolize France, screaming defiance to the nations once subdued, but soon her subduers in turn, giving them plainly to understand that what had once occurred might

No. 40.
EAGLE ALIGHTING.
Bronze. Height, 10 inches.

happen again. A bold, too bold a scheme! Thiers approved, temporized, consulted, dilly-dallied — and finally gave up the plan, alleging that if carried out it would give offense in quarters where France could not afford to offend. The large model of the Eagle of the Grand Army appears to have been utterly lost. The statuette of an eagle with outspread wings on a rock may perhaps be a study for the Grand Army eagle which Barye afterwards wrought out on a small scale. To salve over the disappoint-

ment Thiers gave the sculptor an order for a colossal lion. But about that too the shifty statesman managed to change his mind and the commission was never filled.

This however was not the first scheme for the decoration of the Arc de Triomphe in a grandiose way which came to nothing in the councils of Louis Philippe. A proposal by Chenavard was to treat the arch as Titus did the triumphal arch near the forum at Rome. Napoleon the Great was to stand enthroned on a chariot drawn by a classical span of horses. At the four corners, on horseback however, not on foot like the heirs of Titus, were to be the effigies of Napoleon's brothers and Prince Murat. On the ground about it were to stand the twelve marshals of France like the peers about Charlemagne.

The Salon of 1836 accepted the Seated Lion which was afterwards bought by government and placed in bronze beside the postern of the

Louvre which issues on the quay, but refused all his smaller objects. Some one defined their reason by exclaiming 'this inroad of beasts into sculpture is owing to their easy production and retailing.' Thus Barye had to suffer because men said that his wares were too commercial and savored too much of the shop. We shall presently see that the other or commercial world was equally inimical.

The Lion and Serpent for the Tuileries which was modeled in 1832 shown in plaster in 1833 and cast in bronze by Honoré Gonon and his two sons in 1835 appeared at the Salon of 1836. There was a continuance of attacks from the sculptors and official critics, but the public was delighted and Barye's champions were not idle. One of these remarked: 'The most skillful carver undoubtedly would have failed to translate the thought of the artist with equal fidelity; that is why we are glad this work was not carried out in marble. In M. Barye's manner of working there is a realism in the details which would confound the customary usages of the chisel. When the wax itself has been retouched by the sculptor and metal takes the place of the wax, then the resulting figure preserves all the charm of the clay and seems to have issued fresh from the hands of its author.'

But while these disputes were raging he was conceiving and beginning to formulate the celebrated group Theseus Killing Minotaur. He was also at work on the charming equestrian statuette of General Bonaparte and was able to get it cast by the wax process of Honoré Gonon before the latter died. The rejection of his small pieces seemed to him to prove so rooted a hostility on the part of the Salon that he resolved to do without exhibitions hereafter. That commerce with which he had been taunted should be his salvation. He proposed to eschew the favor of hypocrites who talked of 'grand art' and 'art without thought of gain,' yet all the while were moving heaven and earth to obtain a patron for whose money they were ready to do anything he asked. His workshop should be to him the only exhibition-ground hereafter and his critics those who came with money in poke and a wish to buy in their minds. To this resolve he adhered with characteristic doggedness. After 1837 he never showed a piece in the Salon until the year 1850, when his exhibits must have astonished a great many people whose memories of the Salon fell short of fifteen years.

Unfortunately for Barye he had no rich capitalist who would lend him money to embark as a sculptor of animals for the people and take the chances of the result. A Mæcenas of that sort is in sooth oftener talked about than seriously forthcoming for mention by the truthful muse of history. He needed capital, but could only get it by the usual methods, by making himself responsible for its repayment. Doubtless if he had shared the irresponsible, happy-go-lucky nature of some artists he would have managed to get the money, and if things turned out ill, shrugged his shoulders and left his friends to digest their losses as best might be. But such was not Barye's nature at all. On the contrary he strove with all his might to win the fickle goddess to his side and when she would not he did all in his power to see his creditors righted.

About 1838 he must have first gone into debt. The revolution of 1848 scared the lenders and they demanded repayment which Barye could not then make. When they pressed for payment and insisted there was no escape. All his finished bronzes, all his models and stock in trade went to a founder named Martin, and the sculptor had the bitter grief of knowing that in all probability slovenly, if not altered, statuettes signed with his name, would be sold by the creditors. The reaction that always comes when work of a fine standard is repeated in a poorer style struck not only at the price of his works but at his reputation. It was not till 1857 that Barye finally cleared his skirts of a venture into which pique at the jury of the Salon and a mistaken estimate of his powers as a salesman hurried him.

That melancholy which was noted in him may have taken root during these trying years. One would like to think that the little bronze wolf in the trap, of which we have here an autotype, was his way of expressing what a man of his powers of silence could not give in words. How perfectly he has caught the agony of a beast that never can be tamed,

62

NO. 41.

WOLF CAUGHT IN TRAP

Height 4½ inches

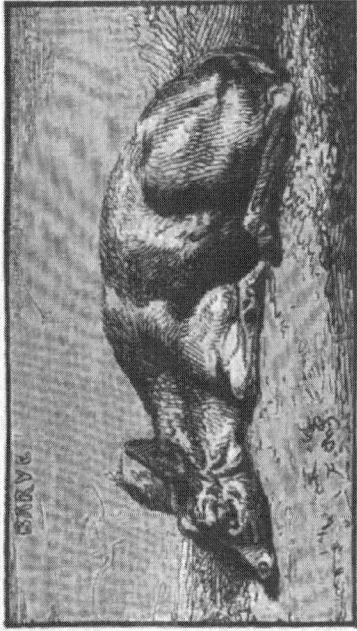

No. 45. FAWN AT REST (etching by C. Jacque).

See No. 15.

as it finds itself rooted to the spot and lifts its head to utter a long dismal howl! Even a wolf can have pathos under Barye's hand.

It was an odd sort of salesman Barye made. Instead of telling the people who came to see him in the out-of-the-way spot where his shop and dwelling were that this or the other piece had been admired by princes and the original or first proof bought by them, he left the visitor to his own devices and appeared more unwilling to part with his bronzes than eager to sell. If the buyer was an amateur he found in the seller a shrewd critic. Often Barye insisted on improvements or a fresh casting of the piece before letting it go.

The financial difficulties in which he presently found himself involved were not lightened by his methods of work. Much thought and many abortive studies for a statuette or a group went to the final result and meantime the business side of his venture languished. He was conscientious to a fault and feared more than anything else that work which was not up to his ideals should leave the shop. Hence negotiations that promised well were sometimes broken off by what appeared mere whim on the part of the sculptor. What the world wants in art as well as literature so called is a staple article which can be furnished in quantity after a demand for it has arisen. Now the smaller bronze articles, having to be repeated almost indefinitely, seem just the things that might be supplied; and so they are if the founder is not pursued by the fear of offering occasionally second-rate work. Barye's bronzes produced in a fine establishment like that of M. Barbédienne are guaranteed by the stamp of that bronze-founder as articles always fully worth their price. But Barye bronzes cast by Barye had a variable element which made some above the average and others below. If no one was keener than the sculptor to perceive what was superior, no one was also more sensitive to what fell below. We find the same thing among the artist artisans of Japan.

Americans in Japan who try to cater to a taste in their countrymen for Japanese articles above the ordinary are met by a singular inability on the part of Japanese artisans to give them in quantity some article of which they have produced an admirable specimen. Say it is an exquisite cup that the intelligent caterer for the home market has discovered. He summons the artisan and makes a contract with him for six dozen such cups with saucers to match, each cup and saucer to be the exact quality of the specimen. The Japanese sucks in his breath, bows to the ground and guarantees that by a certain date they shall be delivered. The day arrives and with it the Oriental. The cups are unpacked—and not one is exactly the same; in the eyes of the American not one is as fine as the specimen cup. The buyer is indignant and refuses to accept them, declaring the bargain null and void according to the words of the contract. The Japanese sucks in his breath, bows to the ground, smiles amicably, packs up his cups and bows himself away. He has done his best. It is the foreigner who demands the impossible because he does not understand the nature of the people and the way of the native workman.

Barye has many points of likeness with the Japanese worker in metals, that marvelous fellow who has produced such wonderful bronzes, often ornamented with a profusion we hold to be lacking in taste, but also at times severe and simple as the best Greek art. It is as if Barye, sprung from the primeval stratum of the population of Europe, a Turanian stratum very near of kin with the main strain in the Japanese compound, had by virtue of that primitive kinship brought forth works of art which have a certain similarity in their mode of genesis with those of the farthest Orient—and a strong inner resemblance so far as an artistic blending in them of realism and impressionism is concerned.

IV

THE years of his abstention from the Salon and endeavor to enter the lists against the practical bronze-founders of Paris were full of labor and successful creations. The Lion Devouring a Doe in the collection of Mr. Cyrus J. Lawrence is dated 1837 and has touches of green patina here and there. As the picture shows, the little object is in one view

horrible, for the lion is all over the poor doe and is hugging her chest into his mouth with a ferocity that makes one's blood run cold. Its tail is raised with an expression of enjoyment such as one sees in the to-and-fro movement of a cat's tail while it crunches a mouse. The mane of the lion is treated in great flocks of hair. The Walters Gallery has a little Listening Stag dated 1838, which is a most charming bit. The stag has the fore feet close together and gazes off with an alert, resolute look. Another stag about the same in size holds one hoof in the air with a most characteristic gesture, ready to give the stamp which shall be the signal to the family for flight just so soon as it shall have decided where the danger lies. A recumbent panther with one paw on a small deer of Java *(Cervus muntjac)* its jaws open in a growl of warning against any beast that shall dispute its prize, will be found among the Lawrence pieces. In the same collection a panther of Tunis walking dated 1840 is remarkable for the thickness of its legs, for in the usual way Barye has adhered to the facts of life rather than sought for grace. The smooth beast crouches on the watch, while its thick tail curls dangerously. To this period belong also the Recumbent Bull seized by a Bear, the Bull on the Defensive and the Rearing Bull, of which the Walters Gallery possesses first proofs. In 1886 the first was sold for $480 and is now much more costly. The bull bellows with pain and strives to rise, but after the nature of his kind must get on its hind legs first. But there the bear has put much of its weight, while teeth and claws are buried in its victim. Yet the latter has plenty of fight left; appearances are by no means all in favor of the bear. No. 1 proof has a fine dark patina. The articulations of the bull's tail and the cording of its muscles are magnificently accentuated.

The acme of the horrible however is reached in a long low bronze dated 1840, of which proof No. 2 is in the Walters collection. Here a python has crushed a doe and is in the act of swallowing it, head foremost. The big eye of the victim glazed in death is just about to slip into enormously extended jaws while its body is still held, but negligently held, in a great fold of the reptile. Barye made a water-color of this tragedy of the forest which luckily fell into the same hands as the bronze and supplies the colors that metals can not give without degenerating into a species of harlequin art we find in the stores for modern bric-à-brac.

In 1846 the group of a Centaur perishing under the hands of a Greek hero was begun and by 1848 it was finished. I shall speak of this later. To the same period belong the specimens in the Walters and Avery collections of a boar, a short spear standing upright in its side. Here also we may place the statuettes of Charles VII 'le victorieux' which M. Barbédienne sells now in two sizes, one very much larger than the model by Barye. Charles VI, Gaston de Foix and the Duke of Orleans are equestrian statuettes of great merit, but not by any means Barye's best. Here we may also place the Rampant Bull pulled down by Tiger, of which Mr. Richard M. Hunt owns a proof, and the bas-relief Lion of the Zodiac so called, for the lower part of the column erected on the site of the Bastille.

This grand lion was thought so well of recently that a plaster-cast was demanded for the Universal Exposition of the present year. The engineer who has charge of the column refused to permit a cast to be made. His reasons are interesting and perhaps instructive for those who own fine bronzes. On the one hand, he maintained that the taking of a cast would in all likelihood injure the bronze by filling up the fine cuts and by scratching the surface; on the other, there would be no knowing what effect it would have on the patina. The finest effects of the bronze, not only those produced by the founder but by the weather, might be ruined forever. This piece is often called the Lion of the Column of July.

During the year 1846 Delacroix painted a beautiful water-color that makes one think of Barye, a lion with a serpent under his claws now in the Walters Gallery. One might imagine it a plagiarism on the Tuileries group, just as one may often be tempted to think that water-colors by Barye were executed under the influence of Delacroix. But we

No. 48. JAGUAR SEIZING ALLIGATOR (front).

Bronze. Height, 3 inches.

are now able to see that each was working independently ever since those
early days when they studied animals side by side in the fair of St.
Cloud and the Jardin des Plantes. The suggestion that Barye was
beholden to Delacroix in anything more than the emulation of comrades
must be absolutely denied.

It is natural that biographers of Barye have placed at the end of their
essays the human figures and groups in which man is the important
factor. Certainly he did make his mark as a sculptor of animals; he
was greatest in the new field which he struck out. But we have seen
that his earliest known work, Milo of Crotona Slain by a Lion, was
better on the human side than the animal. We have noted his busts
and a full-length Saint in early Salons, and then the extraordinarily
able figures of men in some of the table-service groups. Inevitably his
merit as an animal sculptor obscured that as a statuary of men. But
his human figures are many and hardly one of them is insignificant or
undignified. He seems to have ever returned from his studies of beasts
to an unhackneyed, a powerful, a Titanic view of mankind, by exactly
the same process of thought through which those scientific men pass
who approach the study of man's body and his past history on earth by
way of profound researches into the bodily composition and the char-
acters of animals. It was by the constant passage from nature to art and
from art to nature that Barye arrived at such surprising results in the
sculpture of men as well as beasts.

The ancients made fables of various enigmas in the world and gave
them a literary form on the one side and an artistic on the other. It
would puzzle the profoundest antiquarian to say whether myths first
began with a literary or an artistic germ. We may be certain that at an
extremely primitive epoch myths and legends were formed to explain
paintings and sculpture, as well as artistic forms created to embody
myths. The interplay of these two forces resulted in such figures as
Pan of Arcadia and his double, Marsyas of Asia Minor, and the bear-
headed Artemis once worshipped in Attica; also the strange, fantastic
gallery of gods in Egypt, the bull-headed Molochs and the Cherubim

that stood with bodies of lion or bull and heads of men at the portals of Assyrian palaces, together with the eagle-headed adorers of the palm, offering the male element of that beneficent tree in the shape of a cone—a sacred rite which we find carved on a thousand slabs in the ruins of old cities on the Euphrates. Considered in this way some clew is possible through the labyrinths of the Egyptian, Semitic and Greek mythologies which have hitherto remained deeply shrouded in mystery.

Barye was permeated with the scientific spirit of the age but his ideas were necessarily lacking in the clearness they might have gained later in the century, and the forms in which to express them were necessarily limited to those already known and at least partially accepted as beautiful by men of cultivation. He could not very well model an imaginary Missing Link, that figment of a popular misconception regarding theories of evolution. He could not even, by using his knowledge of living animals and the record of extinct forms left in the rocks, create afresh the probable appearance of former denizens of the earth, whether human or not; because to do so would not be art but palæontology. But what he did do on the less artistic side was to advance a step from the combats of wild creatures to the first faint appearance of the subjection of one beast by another for its own profit. He seems to have been thinking of man at an epoch so remote that while he was by no means a monkey, some of the traits now found in the apes had not been eliminated from his nature. He fashioned perhaps his boldest and certainly one of his least beautiful groups, the Ape Riding a Gnu.

The gnu is an African creature which recalls on the one hand the combination of animals found in the art of peoples of Asia Minor and through them the Greeks, such as the Centaur, Chimera, Pegasus, Bucephalus; and on the other the latest doctrines of evolution; because it seems to retain the type of a creature existing in an age when the present types had not been sundered. Its head is that of an antelope, its horns and feet those of cattle, its mane, body and tail those of a

NO. 52.

APE RIDING A GNU

Height 9 inches

horse. With some likelihood the gnu may be considered the origin of the fabled unicorn, which may have been known in Europe only through profile drawings that showed but one of its two horns, and that one apparently jutting from the brow of a slender horse.

Barye has seized on this extraordinary figure, partly because its fine legs and flowing tail make it a graceful object, whatever may be thought of its head; and on its back he placed an ape in the act of essaying to ride. It is a large ape of the chimpanzee variety, which of all the four-handed race is closest to human beings in intelligence. The look of earnest meditation on the ape's face as he attempts this wonderful feat relieves the statuette of any suspicion of the comic. Admirable in its ape-like gravity and signs of thought, the positions of hands and feet are no less characteristic. The long arms reach with ease the tail of the gnu behind and a big lock of the mane in front, thus preventing an upset from the bucking and rearing of the surprised steed. At the same time the other pair of hands, which in us are feet, grip the barrel of the gnu firmly and prevent the ape from slipping to either side.

We have here an object less beautiful, less terrible than the lion smiting a python or the elephant transfixing a tiger with his tusk. It is no longer strength against strength and the weaker to the wall! Here is the reign of brain which has opened that chasm between human beings and beasts, which the ancients after the birth of Christ widened beyond all reason, and which the moderns, Barye among them, have sought to properly estimate and bridge. This neglected statu-ette that few own and still fewer care for, is in some respects quite the most remarkable work that ever emanated from the workshop of Barye's mind. It brings us close up to such pieces as Theseus Slaying Minotaur, begun in 1836, finished several years later, and bought by the govern-ment for the provincial museum at Le Puy, also to Theseus Slaying the Centaur Bianor, called Centaur and Lapith when first designed, and causes us to hark back to the hippogriff in the splendid flying group of Roger Carrying off Angelica belonging to the creative epoch of 1840.

Meantime it may be noted that in 1847 the painter Jeanson succeeded in having the Lion in Repose or Seated Lion, one of the simplest and most majestic pieces by Barye, placed at the entrance to the Louvre from the quay. One lion was not enough; the government demanded of Barye a duplicate to be placed at the other side of the portal. This seemed an artistic heresy which the sculptor could not countenance. For him the only possible comrade for the Lion in Repose would be another figure which might not cheapen its comrade by suggesting an indefinite number of Lions in Repose cast in a mold, and might form an opposite neither too symmetrical nor too different. The lion which is on the left of the gate was cast by the ordinary, not the wax process, and then the duplicate was made for the right side but reversed. Barye used to regard these lions with no little grief, for if one was cast as he would not have cast it, the other seemed to him an outrage. This bronze beast goes by the name of Le Philosophe among the artistic fraternity.

In 1848 M. Ledru Rollin found the opportunity of giving Barye some relief. A curatorship of plaster-casts was vacant and its small salary was a boon to the ill-starred man, to whom a second wife had already presented a large family of children. But let us look at another phase in Barye's development.

V

For the Duke of Montpensier, the youngest son of Louis Philippe, the sculptor made one of his most successful small pieces of beast combat, an Elephant crushing a Tiger. One of the elephant's hind feet is crushing the side of the tiger; another fore foot pins it too, and the head is turned to one side to allow the right tusk to pierce the tiger's neck. The modeling of the great bony framework of the elephant is superb and its concentration of power beyond all praise. For Montpensier he also produced a stately pair of candelabra with the three Graces at the top and the three Goddesses who made of Paris their judge near the foot. Between are three chimeras and at the base three ornamental masks. Part of the same commission was the centre-piece. These candelabra were to light the Roger Carrying off Angelica on the Hippogriff. None

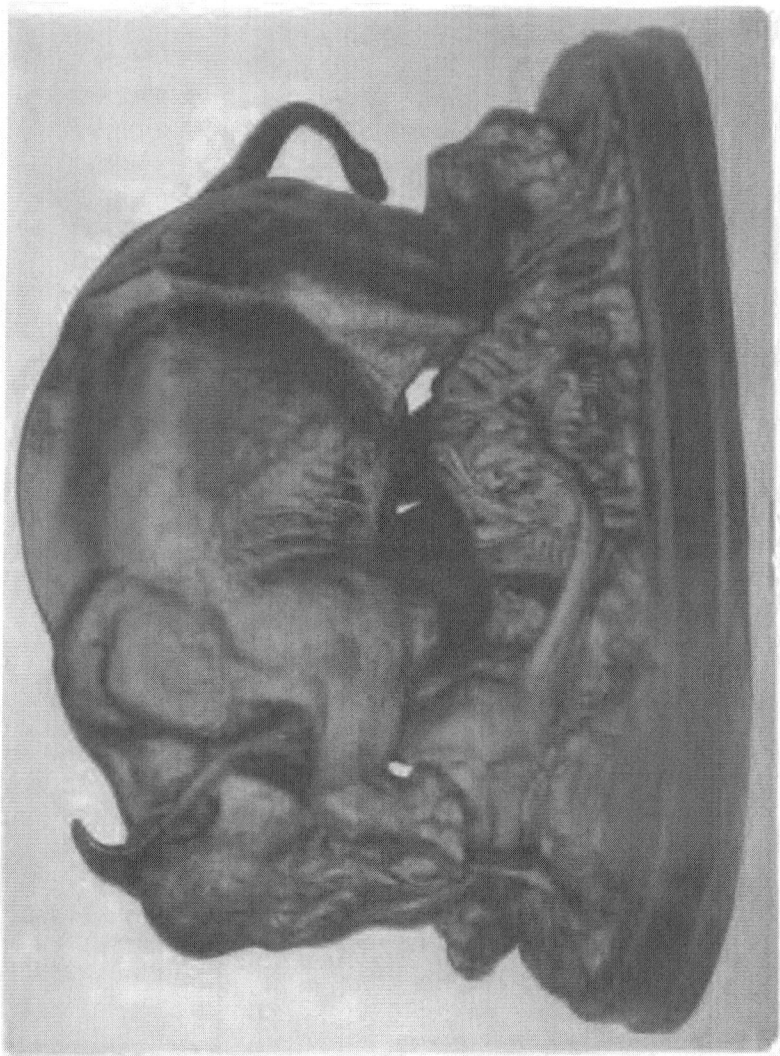

NO. 46.

ASIAN ELEPHANT CRUSHING TIGER

Height 8½ inches

of these pieces were ever exhibited by the sculptor, but they are not unique like the five Hunts for the Duke of Orleans.

The hippogriff exhibits Barye's skill in uniting the characteristics of several creatures. It is a horse-bird upborne on the spray which a dolphin has cast skyward from the sea as it curls itself in a spiral. The ocean sympathizes with the lover and the hippogriff skims the waves with an eager look in its outstretched head like the wise thing it is. Secure on its broad back rides the confounder of magicians, Roger the Paladin, pressing to his steel corslet the bare bosom of the maid he has rescued. The latter is an instance of the purity of Barye's conception of woman, for Ariosto's description of that ride might have warranted a much less delicate treatment. In the mellifluous poem Roger does not act the handsome part and he is well paid for his coarseness. He forgets a certain ring that makes the wearer invisible, but Angelica espies it in time to save herself from a hero who is ready to take advantage of her predicament. The reader may remember how Roger, having turned the Orc or marine monster to stone by the sight of his magic shield, and having taken Angelica the victim thus rescued on his winged steed, was not sufficiently delicate with her, but covered her bosom and eyes with kisses.

> Il destrier punto, ponta i piè all'arena
> E balza in aria, e per le ciel galoppa;
> E porta il cavaliero in su la schiena
> E la donzella dietro in su la groppa.
> Così privò la fera della cena
> Per lei soave e delicata troppa.
> Ruggier si va volgendo, e mille baci
> Figge nel petto e negli occhi vivace.
>
> *Orlando Furioso. Canto X, 112.*

Lovely and tricky Angelica is firm and well-grown in Barye's handling, but not the languishing or voluptuous woman. Roger's hand on her back, as he holds her steady with a light, firm grasp, is a marvelously fine bit of gesture. It is protective and yet tender, but seems to hold her with a respectful touch. There is no caress in it, as if his love for

71

Angelica were more spiritual than fleshly and therefore much finer than Ariosto makes it. The whirling spray and the hard-riding attitude of Roger as well as the direction of Angelica's limbs aid the impression of a tremendous rush through the air.

The hippogriff arose slowly in his mind and its forming may be traced in a little memorandum book now owned by Mr. Geo. A. Lucas of Paris. Olaus Magnus discourses at length on the griffin, maintaining that the ancients conceived it as an enormous eagle to the shoulders, but the rest like a lion, save that its talons were a bird's. We know now that the tusks of mammoths brought from Siberia were thought the claws of this fabulous creature, and conjecture that the tales of the destruction of gold miners and seekers after precious stones it was fabled to make were spread in order to frighten people away from the lands where these are to be found. But some ancient authorities speak of the griffin as a winged horse, and these Barye has followed to great advantage.

Sir John Mandeville believed in the griffin, if not the hippogriff, and explained that it was exactly eight times larger than a lion and could carry off an armed man and his horse in its talons. In some of the old editions of Olaus Magnus we are shown a curious wood-cut of this very feat performed by a lion-bird. The Roc of the Arabian Nights, the now extinct Moa of Australasia, the Phœnix, the Læmmergeyer that is known to carry off young children, and the distorted tales of great animals found in the earth, met together with astronomical and mythological fables to form the hippogriff which Barye has sent careering so blithely across the wave-tops bearing its amorous freight of hero and heroine of romance.

The Nine-Figure Candelabrum which belongs to this romantic bronze is another evidence of Barye's force as a molder of the human figure. But it may be noted that his touch is mediæval rather than modern. It has little of that marvelous deftness we find in the sculpture in vogue nowadays. Rather do the figures impress one with strength and unchangeableness in their author. Barye had enormous versatility in one sense, but he had not quick adaptability to the fashions of the day.

72

That made it unlikely that he should ever amass a fortune. But it was also the balance wheel that prevented him from being driven from his natural path by ideas that contained no sound and living truth.

These candelabra have the Three Graces standing with interlocked arms above the cups for the candles. Below on the shaft are three Renaissance monsters, winged panthers with the breasts of women, and about the lower shaft are the goddesses who have undraped themselves to await the verdict of Paris. With Juno we see the sceptre and peacock; with Venus the dolphin in memory of the birth of Aphrodite from the foam of the sea; with Minerva the owl and sword. The Graces and goddesses are exquisite figures, varied in their poses without seeming to call attention to their pose, and brought into harmonious groups of three. The character of each goddess is expressed by the inclination of each head, the expression of each face and body. Thus Minerva is self-reliant as befits a warrior-maid. Juno sits haughtily with her sceptre touching the ground, her head bent and one wrist resting on her lap. Venus looks out from the group with a direct challenge, twists her body to show herself to advantage and yet clings to Minerva as if she felt in that stern goddess the masculine quality that is wanting to the purely feminine deity of Cyprus. So closely will even a candlestick by Barye bear inspection; and repay it so well.

In the year 1847 he was permitted to decorate the Iena Bridge over the Seine with the large eagles that may still be seen upon it and later it was the Pont Neuf for which he prepared nearly one hundred mascarons or architectural masks. Unexhibited work had been accumulating in his atelier. A predilection for the Bear-Hunt in the sculptor's own mind may account for the fact that during this period he wrought two subsidiary portions of the group into independent statuettes, which teach us to analyze and admire more the component parts of that decoration for the table of the Duke of Orleans. The huntsman on foot who slashes at one of the bears was now cast separately, but in place of a sword he wields a quarter-staff with a vigor that has a parallel in the younger combatant over a game of cards painted by Meissonier in Le Rixe, the famous canvas presented by Louis Napoleon to Queen Victoria and Prince Albert of England. The costumes of the bear hunters are called German of the middle ages. Barye named the statuette Mediæval Peasant. The illustration in autotype is taken from the copy in the Corcoran Gallery which appears to be unique in the United States. Another portion of the Bear-Hunt which may be assigned to this period is the Bear Flying from Three Mastiffs, while the Bear Overthrown by Three Mastiffs which was shown in the Salon of 1833 and will be found earlier in this book in an autotype print is yet one more part of the Bear-Hunt. These are by no means unusual examples of Barye's method in composing and decomposing his groups. The Fawn Couchant and Doe Couchant with Head Erect, which are among the most delightful single pieces, are also found in the Family of Red Deer seen in the fifteenth illustration. We are therefore warranted in the inference that each was modeled separately, and that Barye, after casting the composite piece and finding that it was admired, cast each separately in order to accommodate those buyers whose purses were too empty to indulge in the groups. But there is this also to remember. For many persons the complicated groups are too complicated. Such a tangled skein as the Elk-Hunt affects them unfortunately. They do not like to give the time to unravel the meaning of the group and enjoy the action of so many animals and men in frantic movement. In other words they can thoroughly love and revel in a tune, but are worried by a symphony. With a longer acquaintance this feeling wears off and the large groups win their way to the heart.

The wood-cut of a Jaguar Devouring an Agouti belongs to 1847 or thereabouts. It was fashioned by Barye while he was groping his way toward the Jaguar Devouring a Hare which we shall consider later, and has almost all the marvelous vigor of that marvelous bronze, best seen on this side of the Atlantic in the Walters Collection.

The revolution of 1848 made many changes, but for Barye the most important was the abolition of the jury from the Institute which he

74

No. 57. SEATED LION, CALLED LE PHILOSOPHE, QUAI DU LOUVRE (bronze).

thought, either rightly or wrongly, by intention unfair to him. The Salon of 1850 had a jury composed of artists; it was this jury who accepted the group of Theseus Slaying the Centaur Bianor, or Centaur and Lapith as it was first called. Begun in 1846 it was finished in 1848. The Government bought it, but only to relegate it to the provincial museum at Le Puy, where tourists seldom came and no benefit could accrue for its author by its exhibition. The objection made to a proposition that it should stand enlarged on some public spot in Paris was that it is too mythological! The objection was not serious, or else it was ignorantly made, for Paris like most European capitals swarms with mythological statues of greater or less flatness. The real objection was—people were not prepared for it. There was need of precedents to accustom men to the idea of a statue embodying this particular myth. Without them few amateurs were independent enough to admire a novelty.

In the centaur the sculptor turned to the treasury of Greek myth, as in the Ape Riding a Gnu he had allowed his scientific studies to keep the upper hand. The Centaur is the horseman poeticised; he is the Turkoman who lives on horseback and who terrorized northern Persia until Russia overran his land; the Hun who caused Europe to tremble from end to end. Not only is the centaur a figure which might be expected to appeal to men for whom a classical education is the highest aim, but the composition is far from unknown of a centaur overcome by a bacchanal or a winged genius, if not by a hero. It occurs in a playful variant at least once on walls in Pompeii, where not only the male but the female centaur was a favorite decoration. Barye however did not work from some classical precedent down to modern times, but wrought his modern ideas into forms that assumed classical shapes in order to please the tastes of his educated fellow-countrymen. Hence the Centaur succumbing to the blows of one of the Lapithæ or of their friend Theseus is a fresh creation worked out from original ideas. Had he done otherwise it would not have made the profound impression that stands to its credit.

'What looks like fun, laughter or perhaps the intoxication of love or wine in the famous Centaur of the Capitol, appears a mad struggle for existence in the group by Barye of Theseus Killing the Centaur Bianor. It is the tragic antithesis. The centaurs may be allied in art to the genii *(kerub)* of Mesopotamia, but in history it is likely that they represent a tribe, not a religion; a token, not a faith. When first mentioned the centaurs have no special monster trait. We can see in many early sculptures the gradual evolution of the centaur on Greek soil; first the man being the larger — a monster man with the equine barrel and hind legs added to the complete human figure; then with the horse preponderating, a four-hoofed beast with a human torso in the place of the horse's neck. In the arts we can watch the centaur becoming less and less man, more and more horse, thus corroborating history which does not assign to the centaur tribes physical monstrosity, but savagery and moral depravity. The centaurs in art are curiously parallel to the Asian man-bulls *(kerub)*, and if the meaning of their name as the learned explain it is correct, namely "bull-drivers"— compare the vulgar Western term "cow-punchers"— and later "horse-bull-drivers" (hippocentaurs) it is extremely likely that we owe the centaur of Greek art to a mixture of ideas among the Greeks of the Asia Minor coast. They had seen on the Euphrates, cut in soft stone, the majestic man-bulls, and heard from Greece of the equestrian bull-drivers whose crest was a horse's head. In all probability we have a singular and complete instance of the march of a Semitic art-idea from Asia into Europe, which idea became Aryanized in the process, changing from the bull, more common to Semitic moon-worship (the golden calf, the brazen serpent, Moloch, Astarte, Baal) to the horse, the favorite Aryan symbol of the sun.' *

The Centaur and Lapith as it was first called differs in certain particulars from its secondary form here given and named with more particularity the Combat of Theseus and the Centaur Bianor. In the

* ANTOINE LOUIS BARYE. In The Century Magazine, February, 1886. By HENRY ECKFORD (Charles de Kay).

76

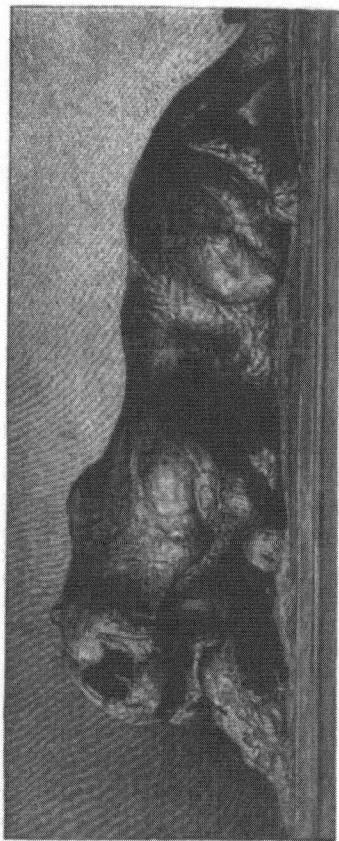

No. 58.   PANTHER DEVOURING AN AGOUTI.
Bronze.   Height, 2⅞ inches.

former state the raised fore-foot of the centaur has hoof and pastern straighter forward and the tail straighter out behind, as if movement had hardly been arrested. The drapery is different and the hair of the centaur's head is less broadly treated than it became later. His left hand, which may be seen clawing the air, was gripped on the Lapith's shoulder and his face expressed less the supreme agony. The Lapith's right knee was pressed to the barrel of the human horse and his left hand instead of pushing the centaur's head grasps his throat. In general it may be said that Barye altered the group by advancing from an earlier stage of the combat to the crisis. The hoofs stumble, the mouth of the centaur is wide in death, the grip of Theseus on his throat appears almost to have done its work and the blow of the rude club on the cranium is all that is necessary to finish a throttled monster. The earlier variant may be detected at a glance by the absence of a clump of cactus which was substituted on the base of the statuette for a rock.

Perhaps nothing shows better the master mind than the ability to alter a successful work without gravely harming it. But a change from some unidentified Lapith in combat with some centaur without name to an individual in the final struggle with a given centaur was in the right direction. The hero being god-like Theseus, there must be no question how the battle is going. Bianor can not be carrying him off; for such children of the sun as Theseus cannot be shown in a doubtful situation when their hour of triumph arrives; nor can the sometimes beneficent, but generally baleful demons of the earth (kerubs and centaurs) be depicted otherwise than succumbing to their heavenly foes.

An examination of the Theseus Slaying Bianor at the Metropolitan Museum, an enlarged bronze from the workshop of Barye himself, will repay a visit. One should bear in mind the Ape Riding a Gnu and compare the different ways in which Barye has shown, on the one hand the first glimmer of an idea of subjecting animals for use, and on the other the complete control of an animal-man by the most perfected human being. Theseus uses his feet to maintain his hold, digging the big toe into the hollow before the centaur's flank; but how differently does the ape balance himself on the gnu, also employing the toes to keep itself secure! Théophile Gautier remarked: 'People are astonished because a sculptor who modeled animals so well made such a success when he fashioned men and heroes, just as if the form were not the same under all its apparent diversity; as if it could have any secrets hidden from a thinker gifted with an eye as piercing as Barye's.'

At this late day France could not do better than erect a Theseus Slaying Bianor in bronze the size of life or of heroic proportions, cast by the wax process or as Gustave Planche suggested in marble. It should stand somewhere in the Tuileries gardens in memory of the sculptor. Not that in the present day great sculptors are lacking. When M. de Nieuwerkercke was placed by Napoleon III in charge of the Louvre he displaced Barye from his position and gave his modest salary to M. Frémiet, the sculptor of that charming little Joan of Arc who sits so innocent and resolute, high on her saddle on the Place des Pyramides. Frémiet is still alive and Falguière, Chapu, Dubois, Saint Marceaux and Rodin, to speak of no others, maintain France at the head of all nations in sculpture. But among them there is no Barye and his statuettes have luckily the very qualities which fit them for colossal enlargement or to the size of life.

It is true that the Centaur group does not possess that repose which we generally demand of public monuments. But it may be observed that the rule of repose is not a rigid one and may in some cases be departed from with advantage. There is a field in sculpture for the most violent action, provided the moment chosen is one of suspended movement and the subject demands a lively treatment. Préault, Rude, Rodin and other masters have violated a sound general rule and justified their departure by success.

It is however certain that such groups are proper neither for a very high pedestal, nor for a lofty perch on the front of a building such as was unluckily accorded to some of Barye's groups in stone. We

No. 60. THESEUS SLAYING THE CENTAUR BIANOR.
Bronze. Height, 50 inches.

No. 63. HUNT OF THE TIGER (from right).

must be on a level with the centaur to appreciate the muscular effects in the monster stumbling to his death, the stern impassive face of his executioner and the play of the dying centaur's hands, which are perhaps the most expressive points in the work. Barye's profound knowledge of the human figure, denied him during his life, but visible as we have seen in his very earliest work, is nowhere more apparent than in Theseus and the human half of Bianor. The difficult feat of representing, without a shock to our unaccustomed eyes, the place of juncture between the man's torso and that of the horse is accomplished with apparent ease. The lower part of the hero's figure fills up and conceals the broad planes of the human and equine backs, and prevents the uncomfortable effect which may be felt when we regard a centaur without a rider in Greek sculpture. The curved left fore leg and tail bring the composition more together than appears to be the case with the original form, while the drapery falling from the back on the cactus and flowing on the ground between the hind hoofs gives a sinuous line that keeps the whole from too much angularity, in view of the centaur's sharply bent knee and pointed right elbow together with the right elbow of Theseus himself. The popularity of this group since Barye's death may be inferred from the fact that M. Barbédienne offers it in four different sizes and a first sketch, one of them costing 6000 francs.

It has the honor of creating one of the most pertinacious and picturesque legends-that wove themselves round Barye as the victim of poverty. According to this tale the sculptor was so poor that he was forced to retail his statuettes from house to house like the Italians who from rude molds fashion little images of the most execrable modeling, and placing a dozen on a board parade the streets with their fragile wares. Barye going the rounds of the jewelers and vendors of knick-knacks for the parlor with a Theseus Slaying Bianor balanced on his head is one of those dramatic points which van Mander, Vasari and Lanzi would have loved. There is however nothing to sustain it.

In attempting this subject Barye had the ancient centaurs to compete with and to avoid, though to do so was to imply that he could improve on the Elgin marbles in the British Museum. He had also the Theseus Slaying a Centaur at Vienna by Canova as a rival, but that gave him little trouble. Canova modeled a very ogre of a Theseus who towers above a poor little centaur and by merely touching him makes the man-horse fall on his knees. As no physical power could have produced this result, Theseus standing where he does, we must infer that Theseus 'eyed him over' first and then dispatched him at his leisure. Needless to say that our sympathies are with the little centaur and that we regard the big human bully with contempt. Canova may have precedents in this treatment of the combat, but there are many statues, reliefs and paintings from antiquity which cannot be followed with success.

In the artistic realm Barye's Centaur is an advance on that of Greece. In the scientific realm the group shows the conquest of simpler, more specialized forms over the complex monsters of the past in the struggle for existence.

No. 64.   THESEUS SLAYING MINOTAUR.
Bronze. Height, 18 inches.

CHAPTER FOUR

I

ROM the year 1850 onward Barye began to have some reward for years of laborious silence. He had early known the bitterness of seeing men like Fratin and Fauginet preferred, though of course he estimated rightly his own superiority. We are sure that he regarded as less unjust the partiality of the public for the highly finished bronzes of Mêne, for these are real works of art only second to Barye's. Besides, there is a lithograph of a lioness and cubs made by Barye, a proof of which bears a dedication to Mêne. If we call the latter's the product of genius, the bronzes by Mêne may be considered the work of a highly talented sculptor. Barye could not have ignored the distinguished merits of Cain and of Frémiet, his successor at the Jardin des Plantes. M. Cain, whose large bronzes stand in the Tuileries gardens, owns many Barye water-colors and lithographs.

Barye was Professor at the Jardin, but seems to have been ill-adapted for the position. He lectured at times, but had little power of interesting his pupils and for the most part contented himself with looking over the work of those who frequented the establishment and occasionally vouchsafing a remark. The habit of silence, for which he had been rallied at the dinners of a circle of clever fellows or at the cafés, grew on him as he became more and more involved in disastrous affairs and experienced the neglect or the attacks of the indifferent or the envious. He seemed to wear a padlock on his lips, was the remark of an acquaintance. The justice of the sally is perceived in all his portraits, which show lips pushed together resolutely.

This look is probably the main basis for a number of anecdotes, which if true would argue Barye a bear indeed, nay, a man whose temper was so ungoverned that he was ready to assail a patron on the slightest grounds of offense, at the mere suspicion of a criticism upon a design or model. That he was impatient of babblers and those who spend the time of busy men without having a purpose is more than likely. But good judges who saw much of Barye during the last twenty years of his life give emphatic denial to this view of his character or manners. They represent him as reserved to a degree unusual among Frenchmen, but courteous, and before everything dignified; talkative enough when under four eyes, but not a person to contribute to the general pleasure of a dinner-table. It is probable that while Barye was naturally taciturn his reserve was increased by a consciousness of defective education in early life. To the same cause we may attribute his dislike of writing letters, in consequence of which most of his correspondence was conducted by his wife or one of his daughters.

Almost the only instance on record to which credence may be given, when Barye uttered a complaint or said a harsh thing of those who misunderstood his work or understood its greatness too well for their own peace of mind, is preserved by Théophile Silvestre. Perhaps provoked to it by the warmth of his friend's indignation, and turning over in his mind all the miserable tricks of which he had been a victim, but especially that which consisted in keeping him down with a nickname, Barye said: 'In fobbing me off among the animals to get rid of me, my contemporaries have ranged themselves below the beasts.'

The Salon of 1851 accepted another group which approaches nearer the ordinary ideals of a grand statue for public places. It was conceived

No. 65. BRONZE BUST OF BARYE by Moulin.
Height, 23 inches.

as far back as 1841. Again it is Theseus whom he chooses and again he depicts the godlike hero destroying a monster. But the latter has in Greek mythology no good side like that shown by at least one of the centaurs, Chiron, who was the instructor of the demi-gods while young. The Minotaur is a representative of the evil spirits of the grave who rise to prey on the living, of the terror that lurks in the night when the sun is absent, and seems, to the childlike imagination of primitive men, to have gone perhaps forever. In closer connection with the history of religions, he represents early Semitic faiths based upon such panic fears as existed along with gorgeous rituals and ceremonies ruthless in their cruelty among the Phœnicians and Jews, when the latter passed their first-born through the fire or into the red-hot arms and flaming belly of Moloch.

'Instead of considering Minotaur the product of licentious imaginations run wild,' to quote again from the article in The Century Magazine, 'or the caricature of an early tyrant who exacted slaves as tribute from Attica, or the symbol of the junction in Crete of two warring religions, or a special emblem of the god of the sun, we can now ally him with such genii *(jinn)*, as the wardens of the portals in Babylonia and Assyria and like them consider him the idol of a subjugated people, the sign of a religion relegated to the second place. We can be as confident as possible that Theseus himself was a pure sun-god humanized, like Hercules, Bellerophon and Perseus. He makes war on and subdues a monster who bears the root of the word "moon" in his name. As it was suggested long ago, Minotaur means the moon and the beast sacred to the moon. Theseus overwhelms him just as the rising sun causes the moon to fade. The labyrinth in which he wanders is the dark world under the flat earth—Hades. The boys and maidens dedicate to him are the human sacrifices his rites demanded which the new religion puts an end to. In many other places besides Crete sun-worship drove out moon-worship with its horrid rites of Moloch. Thus Minotaur belongs with Gorgon, Typhon, the Titans, Giants, Cyclopes, among the gods of a dark past and lower civilization. By a further move back into the past these composites of animals and men connect themselves with totems or the animal badges assumed as crests or emblems by families, tribes and nations.'

The Minotaur infested the labyrinth, that singular fancy which appears on coins of Crete five hundred years before Christ and is still to be found as a sort of practical joke in gardens of France and England wrought out in high hedges of evergreen. The labyrinth of the under world in which the sun wanders at night had a parallel above men's heads in the stars which suggest a labyrinth in which a spirit might well be puzzled to find its way. When we were considering the northern worship of the bear, we found that there was just such alternate glancing of thought from the animal famous for its courage and magical properties on earth to the Great Bear, the wonder-working constellation that swings in the sky.

So the Minotaur myth is a resultant of various ideas that embraced heaven and earth alternately until they issued in a strange, and to our thought repulsive, myth. It has puzzled archæologists to assign to Minos and Pasiphaë, the father and mother of Minotaur, their proper place as symbols of heavenly bodies, because their respective sexes do not agree with the ordinary view of sun and moon. But if we remember that the Germans retain the ancient idea of the sun as a woman which we find among the Lapps and Japanese we have the clew. Minos is the moon in its male form. Pasiphaë (all-shiner) is the sun in its female form. Minotaur is their offspring and has like its father the ideas of night, demoniac powers and the labyrinths of the under world and the starry sky connected with it. Phœnician in origin, the sacrifices of children to the horned moon-god come to an end when Theseus, the male sun-god of a higher race represented by the Greeks proper, makes his way through the labyrinth of night and destroys the demon of darkness. As the Greek influence predominated the gods which could be identified with another race were forced into repulsive and degraded forms.

The Minotaur occurs on coins of Cnossus, once a flourishing com-

NO. 67.

PANTHER SEIZING STAG

Height 15 inches

mercial city on the northern coast of Crete. He has a human form, but a bull's head, the horns recalling the moon when at the crescent, exactly as in the case of Diana, the female moon, according to ideas more purely Greek. He is shown running or kneeling and holds in each hand a large globe, for which reason Minotaur has been mistaken hitherto for a sun-god, together with the fact that on the same coin but on the opposite face the picture of the labyrinth is completed by a swastika or four-leg, which is generally a sign of the sun. The globes in the hands of the running Minotaur however may be considered to mean the stealing of the world of light by the demon of the dark; the sun-emblem on the labyrinth merely represents Theseus. On later coins we have a naked youth seated on a labyrinth and carrying in one hand a Victory, who must be Theseus. Thus we get the chain of evidence complete that Theseus is a variant on the sun-god, male as to sex, while Minotaur is a variant on the moon-god, and also male like his father Minos.

Such confusion resulting from the habit of antique nations of imagining their gods in married pairs and then exalting one of the couple so high that the other is forgot belongs to nearly every religion on earth. We are also constantly meeting with the degradation of gods belonging to a conquered race into positions of subserviency. It often seems as if the conquerors wished to perpetuate the memory of such great changes in the political world among peoples ignorant of writing save in the rudest ways, using monuments exactly as the Egyptians used their hieroglyphs, namely as a means of preventing entire forgetfulness of past events. Thus the Minotaur-Theseus combat, when explained by the teachers of the inner meaning of monuments, would embody the fusion of a Phœnician and an Aryan-Greek religion. The combat of centaurs and Lapiths however might have been meant to recall the enfranchisement of the Greeks proper from dominion exercised by the horse-tribes of Thessaly or of the Asian steppes before they had completely occupied the land which we call Greece.

There is, indeed, a strong parallel between the Centaur group and that of the Minotaur as composed by Barye. One is the concentrated epic of the warfare between two races or civilizations, the other between two religions. The Minotaur group is the simpler, and yet its myth is more profound. That group also, although given to the world after the Centaur, was really conceived and substantially finished before the other. In some respects it is also the finer of the two statuettes.

It seems natural now to us that Barye should have advanced from his combats of animals to combats of heroes against monsters. But if natural and easy, why did not others do it before him? In other words, now that Barye has been accepted, we are in danger of forgetting how courageous he was to step out of the common line of classical subjects and treat those which were practically unstamped by the approval of the scholars and connoisseurs of the past. Only by keeping this before our minds can we estimate properly the genius of Barye. He first created a new department for the exercise of artistic talents, and then, not content with a glory such as only the rarest artists attain, pushed forward into a field hitherto held by the greatest of Greek sculptors. Had Theseus and the Centaur, or Theseus and Minotaur, been dug up at Pompeii or Olympia, every archæological and art magazine in the world would have had its portrait and expatiated on its magnificent Greekness. Every museum would have sent for casts and lecturers would have pointed out wherein the moderns lagged far behind the ancients, namely in the wonderfully fresh way the real was blent with the ideal. It only falls short of the very greatest sculpture known by having in a less degree than a certain few statues that bright and godlike serenity we find in the Venus of Melos.

Theseus and Minotaur has the highest qualities for monumental effect. It is calm and noble without pushing nobility to the point of superhuman power. Thus the hero is not a magician or a god from the point of whose sword issues a force that slays the demon, neither is he a man doing easily what no man could. He is a powerful hero by reason of his mind, which has trained his body so that it can defeat untrained brawn and muscle, mind which has dug the copper and tin and cast the bronze sword to aid him in the struggle against the brute forces of

No. 61. HEAD OF SEATED LION (front).

No. 62. HEAD OF SEATED LION (profile).

nature. His stride keeps him erect against the heavy onslaught of the
bull-man and he prevents the latter from throwing him by seizing one
great bovine ear and forcing the monster back of the perpendicular.
In vain does the latter strike with his left leg behind the hero's right
knee at the spot the wrestler tries to hit in order to bring his opponent
down; in vain he clutches the latter's body with both hands in the effort
to get a lock round the torso. Theseus holds him off just where he
wants him and pauses coolly to select the exact spot where he will bury
his blade half-way to the hilt. So the matador pauses coolly before he
thrusts his sword into the neck of the bull—then to wipe the blade carefully on his brilliant kerchief and turning, salute the spectators with an
air of dignity from which he strives to eliminate every trace of pride.

As in the Centaur group so here, the hero wins with his brains, not his
brawn, having mastered his foe before administering the fatal stroke.
Once more we see in perfect fusion the two dominant elements in
Barye, so marvelous in the most educated and deeply read man, but far
more wonderful in one who was sent almost without schooling into the
workshop while a little boy. These elements we have traced before:
they are the artistic that makes a thing of beauty out of a tragic and
even ghastly subject, and the scientific that digests and turns into
symbols the greatest of questions, the past on earth of animals and man.
The way in which he has carried the human back upward into the tremendous neck of the bull and downward into the coarse bovine tail, the
latter seeming to spring naturally by powerful roots from the flanks,
so that it is not a mere appendage like the horse-tails of satyrs, but a
part of the monster that might be switched in all directions, is certainly
a marvelous feat of imagination in sculpture.

But such are all the combats of animals that went before. Where
and when could Barye have seen animals in conflict? In some cases he
fell into geographical mistakes or deliberately made anatopisms, if the
coinage of a word be forgiven. A tiger may be seen devouring an animal that does not exist in that part of the world where tigers are found.
The bear of one continent is put in conflict with that of another. The

Jaguar Devouring an Alligator was entered on Barye's own catalogue Jaguar Devouring a Crocodile. Yet jaguars are only found in America while crocodiles are not. We have only the alligator in a few varieties. Here Barye yielded to the necessities of the case. He modeled a true alligator with its short snout and half-webbed hind feet, but instead of *caiman* the ordinary term in French, he used the word everybody understood, crocodile, though strictly speaking it was a misnomer.

Hardly ever could he have seen captive wild beasts fighting with each other. Barye did not live in Roman times when the wild beasts of three continents were brought to the Eternal City and pitted against each other in the arena. Nor did he travel. It is not known that he ever left France; probably he never saw much of his own country. He was a Parisian though so un-Parisian. It was sheer imagination therefore that enabled him to construct in his own mind a picture of what a vast number of animals must have looked like, had a chance encounter or the ever-present law of hunger brought them together in a struggle where the weaker must succumb. It looks so easy—but how could he have done it unless he saw them in the act with his own eyes? To ask the question is to assert that their maker is a genius.

II

THÉOPHILE SILVESTRE published a very appreciative essay on Barye in his Histoire des Artistes Vivantes which appeared in 1856 with a portrait by Flameng on steel which has been retouched by that etcher for our frontispiece. The year before an English observer, Bayle St. John, called attention to his merits in The Louvre, a work published at London by Chapman and Hall. 'M. Barye is assuredly one of the greatest artists that France possesses' he wrote; 'one of those also who have been most roughly tried in the course of a life fertile in masterpieces of a deep and enduring character.' The death in 1855 of the sculptor Rude who composed the only brilliant reliefs for the Arc de Triomphe and also contributed groups full of audacity and fire to the

NO. 68

MOUNTED ARABS KILLING LION

Height 14½ inches

decorations of the Louvre must have made people think that Barye too was growing old. But the article by Gustave Planche in the July issue of the Revue des deux Mondes of 1851 brought him first before the scholars and connoisseurs of France. These owe that acute and valiant critic much for constituting himself the life-long champion of an artist who could not or would not advance his own interests by intrigues and prayers.

The following year the Salon accepted a Jaguar Devouring a Hare which contains that ferocity and that gluttonous enjoyment of its prey we find in all the cat tribe. The modeling of the jaguar's shoulders and head was of the broadest, so that it bespoke a great change in the standards the jury kept before them that the group was entered at all. But it was not only a public success; the government bought it for the Luxenbourg collection, whence it has been removed to the Louvre. 'How many times' wrote M. Bonnat the painter recently 'have I gone to the Luxembourg merely to see his Jaguar Devouring a Hare! How often I have crossed the Tuileries in order to look at the talons of his Lion and Serpent—those tragic talons so marvelously analyzed and modeled!'

Owing to the absence of color and the similarity in shape of the big cats this jaguar is sometimes called a tiger, though anybody well acquainted with wild beasts would not fail to note the difference in the growth of fur about their respective heads. The last biographer of Barye has made a worse mistake in calling a magnificent Walking Tiger a lioness, although the sculptor marked very plainly in the bronze the vertical or sloping stripes which identify the living animal at once. Barye has resorted to this method in other cases, most notably however with leopards and ocelots whose 'eyes' in the fur are sometimes recorded by two shallow circles, one within the other.

The Jaguar and Hare represents the whole family of the felines at their repasts with the possible exception of the lion, especially their constant watchfulness both for the inroads of other animals and their own species and for another chance to seize a prey. There is an insatiable lust for blood among these creatures which is found in the domestic cat as well as the tiger. The good mouser is not content with as many mice as will make a meal, but hastens to kill one and catch another as long as any are within reach. So the tiger, unless old, will slaughter a whole flock of sheep though it can not carry away or eat more than two at the most.

The jaguar has commenced, as all the carnivora do, at the entrails of the hare and eats the softer parts first.   But meantime it watches keenly for interruptions or another victim, laying its ears well back in sign of readiness to dispute its meal with anything that comes near. In many parts of America the jaguar at its meal is surrounded by birds that feed on carrion and will sometimes venture very close in hopes to steal a bit.   In this jaguar Barye has caught exactly that alert look, in addition to the expression of head and tail which betokens enjoyment of a prey still hot with its life-blood.

The history of this group in the auction room shows the rapid advance in cost of prime works by Barye. At the sale of the sculptor's models and statuettes after his death M. Sichel bought the copy now in the Walters Gallery for $580.   Ten years later at the Sichel sale Mr. Walters paid for it $1880.   Last year M. Bonnat the painter paid for a copy no better than this the round sum of $5000.

It may be noted that Barye's case was externally like Millet's. Neglected while alive and ready to sell his work at low prices, there needed but his death to cause people, who had seen him extolled unmoved, while he was still producing, to discover that he was a genius and strive for his works.   Copies could still be issued but no more proofs bearing the unmistakable touch of the master.

I say externally, but in truth there was a deep radical correspondence between Millet and Barye that extended beyond their origin in the same lower middle class, the one a superior peasant, the other a superior burgher. For if Millet was deeply impressed by the monotonous gloomy life of peasants and dared to paint them, Barye was moved by the dumb creatures of the world and lifted them into good

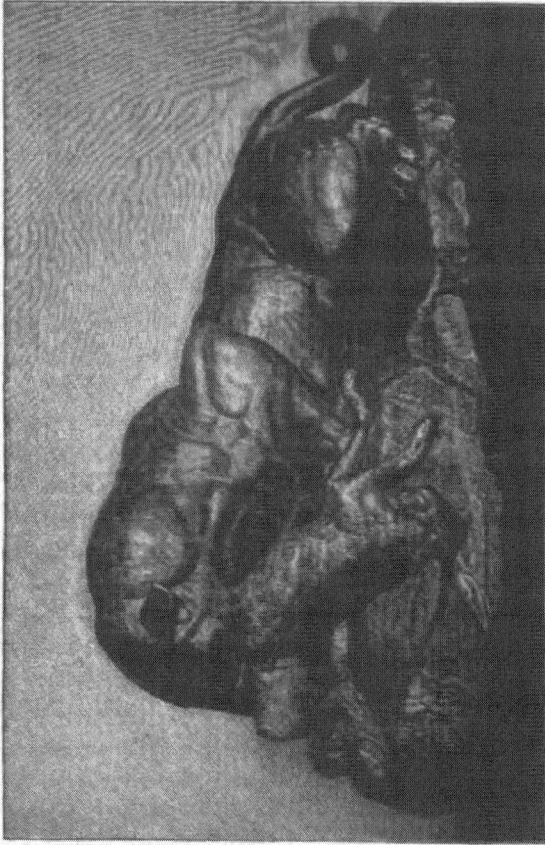

No. 59. JAGUAR DEVOURING A HARE.

Bronze in the Louvre. Height, 15½ inches.

human society. Both suffered for audacity in proposing a new order
of things which they knew to be art, but which arbiters of the arts
considered poor and unfinished work. Millet's painting was and
still is charged with being muddy and 'cottony' while his subjects
were called vulgar. Barye's modeling was thought hurried and unfinished, while his subjects were chiefly beasts regarded by men as
peculiarly his foes, or at the least animals without the stamp of approval from the ancients.

It has been observed that the ordinary Frenchman appears singularly
obtuse to the sufferings of domestic animals, often treating them with
a brutality that seems to spring from ignorance as much as anything.
In fact until recently the whole world failed to appreciate that beasts
have feelings and should be treated with kindness. Fifty years ago
there was far more indifference, ignorance and cruelty to animals than
we can well imagine at the present day. By familiarizing people
with the beauty of wild beasts and even of strange, uncanny creatures,
the way opened for improvement in this regard. Barye has helped
by indirect but efficient means to raise the status of the brutes, just as
Millet has raised the status of the peasant who toils for his daily bread.
His bronzes might well decorate the offices of the various societies for
the prevention of cruelty to animals.

Who indeed has approached him in the grandeur that he gave to
the larger, and as we express it, nobler of the wild beasts? He made
rabbits in bronze that raise one's respect for bunny. The tortoise, the
civet cat, even such an odd figure as the honey-eating badger of Africa
assume a certain dignity under his magic touch. But what shall any
one say to describe the disdainful majesty of the Walking Tiger, one of
the first illustrations of this book? We must go to William Blake to
find a seer like Barye.

Tiger, tiger, burning bright
In the forest of the night,
What immortal hand or eye
Framed thy fearful symmetry?

91

In what distant deeps or skies
Burned that fire within thine eyes ?
On what wings dared he aspire ?
What the hand dared seize the fire ?

And what shoulder and what art
Could twist the sinews of thy heart ?
When thy heart began to beat
What dread hand formed thy dread feet ?

What the hammer, what the chain,
Knit thy strength and forged thy brain ?
What the anvil ? what dread grasp
Dared thy deadly terrors clasp ?

When the stars threw down their spears
And watered heaven with their tears
Did He smile His work to see ?
Did He who made the lamb make thee ?

III

THE Empire was declared in 1852 and the new potentate, dreaming of Charlemagne and Napoleon the Great, married the beautiful and charming young Spaniard who did so much to render his reign one of magnificence and taste. Among the artists who were more or less patronized under Napoleon III was Barye, his genius being enough understood to bring him orders, though usually the latter were not such as to evoke his finest powers.

In 1853 the Duchess of Orleans, her husband killed by an accident, her father-in-law the king in exile, sold the famous table ornaments and dispersed its several members to the four winds, not, let us hope, to remain forever apart. Strange to say the Bear Hunt was the piece for which bidders ventured highest. It fell at $2420. The Elk Hunt came next for $980; then the Wild Bull Hunt to Lutteroth for $900, and Prince Demidoff was able to secure the magnificent Tiger Hunt with Elephant for $820. The Lion Hunt brought only $600. It would not be safe to conjecture what pieces without duplicates such as these

No. 70. A. L. BARYE WITH CENTAUR GROUP. (From a Photograph.)

would bring if they were now offered for sale. But it is not likely that at the present time the Tiger Hunt would stand in point of price fourth. Notable is the fact that the hunts of European animals brought the best prices in 1853. The same peculiarity is seen in the four smaller beast combats in the set. The Eagle and Bouquetin fetched a much higher price than the groups in which the leopard, bison or gnu, and lion figure.

Perhaps the sale recalled Barye to the authorities and enabled some of his friends among the artists to secure for him in 1854 a professorship at the Jardin des Plantes. Barye was. a great favorite in spite of his reserved manners and chariness of speech. Those who knew him, those who listened to his lectures at the Jardin, found him the pleasantest, most kindly, most courteous of men. The tales to the contrary are pure concoctions due to the necessity many people are under to tell a good story and make it picturesque, whatever betide. Harsh, mournful, sharp-spoken men do not receive the praise Barye got, nor do their friends bestir themselves to lobby in their interests for a place to keep them out of want. To match our frontispiece, here is a written sketch by Silvestre which describes Barye at this point in his life, namely the year 1855.

'He is fifty-nine years old, and of a size above the middle height. His dress is careful, without extravagance or foppery. His manner and gestures are precise, correct, quiet and dignified; and he brings into conversation nothing that is dry, or flabby, or pedantic. His watchful straightforward eyes look you always in the face frankly and profoundly, neither with a provoking stare nor with impertinence. His brow is losing its short and whitening hair; his nose is slightly turned up; the planes of the face are strongly carved and united by delicate modeling. Barye observes you and waits, listens to you with singular patience and penetrates your character without fail. The most stubborn melancholy and the most concentrated self-respect escape as if without his knowledge from the depths of his thought and show themselves on a face which is of a clear, transparent tone.'

In 1855 occurred the Universal Exposition, a pale thing compared with that of the present year, but fraught with benefit to many men. Barye received the Grand Medal of Honor in the section of artistic bronzes. Then too he obtained the officer's cross in the Legion of Honor. A little ease began to show itself in the pinched circumstances of a man with many children and a proved inability to sell his wares. But what was more to his taste, honors began to fall to him in recompense for all his troubles. We may hope that these did something to remove that melancholy which seemed to Silvestre so stubborn.

At this time he lived in the Rue Montagne Sainte Geneviève, but kept his old residence in the Marais quarter, Rue Saint Anastase, for his workshop and store. There in 1855 he had for sale more than a hundred different bronzes ranging in size from a turtle only two centimeters high and six long, fit to be worn as a locket, up to the big bronze of Roger and Angelica on the Hippogriff, fifty-three centimeters by sixty-seven, which is a good lift for a man. The prices at which he sold these things appear comic at the present day when Europe and America are scoured for pieces on which he lavished care—and also unfortunately infected with reproductions, some of them secret and fraudulent, others openly manufactured and sold under the protection of the law. It should be remembered to the credit of M. Barbédienne of Paris that, while he makes the best of all reproductions of Barye's bronzes, having bought at the sale after the sculptor's death a great many models and originals, yet he also takes pains to show on each bronze in the plainest possible fashion that his are not originals but copies. A round brass stamp will be found inserted in all such bronzes, making it impossible for the ignorant or the dishonest to sell one for Barye's handiwork.

Barye did not meet with such scrupulousness often, for it is said that one member of his own household was base enough to palm off wretched pieces on the world, thus stabbing the father in his most sensitive place. A founder who obtained possession of models by Barye issued a great quantity of poor things and the sculptor was not able legally to stop

NO. 71.

TARTAR WARRIOR CHECKING HORSE.

Height 13½ inches

it. Another fabricator however, not protected by law, was caught at his tricks and his shop seized by the police. In foreign countries Barye's animals have been copied right and left for such iron lions and dogs as some people buy at the weight in metal for the decoration of their gardens. It may be said, however, that in these extreme cases the workmanship was bad that no reflection was cast on the originator.

Not so with the Parisian copies, legal and illegal. They are still a trouble, because they give themselves out for Barye bronzes and are readily mistaken for the best by persons who have no little artistic taste but happen never to have studied bronzes enough to guard them from mistakes. In such matters people are no more to be blamed than they are for mistaking poor copies of paintings for old masters. No one can be a judge by natural superiority alone. Those who know most of old paintings and bronzes are the least ready to decide off-hand the genuineness of a given piece.

At this period Barye sold a small rabbit, without base, for half a dollar, the little turtle for sixty cents, and the Hippogriff for $140. No single piece cost more than this. The grand candelabrum covered with figures and decorative monsters cost $200 the pair; and another with ten figures $280. These were the highest prices he asked, nor was it possible for him to raise his demands much during the twenty years that remained to him of life.

Yet there was some improvement from the fact that he did make sales. Strange to say, it was to Americans rather than to his own people, to curious citizens of the United States poking about in odd corners of the old country, delighted to discover things that do not exist at home, and bringing with them, hidden under the exterior of indifference for which they are blamed, a fresh way of looking at art as well as questions of society and politics. The painter William M. Hunt was an admirer of Barye, bought many pieces and urged his friends from Boston and New York to acquire them.

Mr. William T. Walters of Baltimore was a visitor to the dingy little shop, Quai des Célestins, as early as 1859. While the civil war raged he remained in Paris, often shipping Barye bronzes as presents to his friends at home, some of whom were by no means cultivated enough in the 'section of artistic bronzes' to appreciate what they had received. One of the pains of the discoverer consists in having the teeth of his gift horses examined with scant courtesy. The nucleus of the collection in the Corcoran was now bought by Mr. Walters. Mr. Richard M. Hunt the architect followed the lectures of Barye at the Jardin des Plantes in 1861, modeling various animal figures under his supervision, and became not only a focus of enthusiasm regarding his works, but a warm admirer of the kindly, firm-lipped old man. Others sought out a sculptor who could, as they perceived when visiting the Tuileries and Luxembourg, model wild beasts at two extremes of passion like the Jaguar Devouring the Hare or Lion and Serpent, and the Seated Lion of the Louvre wicket. Like so many another French artist, Barye began to realize that if his countrymen did not value him at his worth, the world after all is not limited to Paris, nor even to France — a thought difficult to bring to any sort of quickened consciousness in the mind of a Frenchman.

Barye was like Rousseau a confirmed home-stayer. There is no record of his having ever left his native land, not even when a soldier, and the chances are strongly in favor of this singular phenomenon — that the sculptor of deadly combats between wild beasts in Africa, Asia, the tropics and the Arctic Circle never went further from Paris than the village of Barbizon.

The fact may be used as an argument against Barye on the score that one who has not studied wild animals in freedom can not really understand them and give their true movement. On the other hand it may be said that one should not derogate from an artist's work because he has not performed the impossible. There is no known way for an artist to observe the carnivora in freedom unless he goes to enormous expense. Should he imitate the method of catching leopards and lions depicted by an ancient artist on the walls of a grand tomb discovered near Rome some centuries ago, he would not be much better off, and

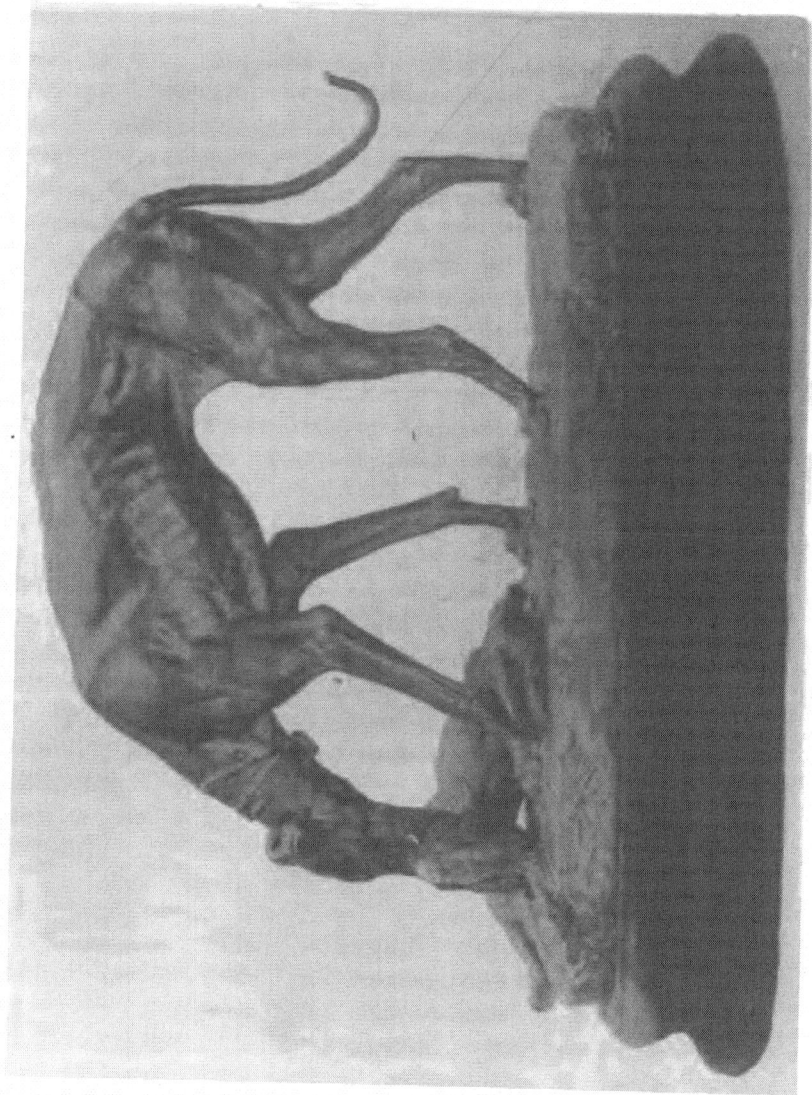

NO 72

GREYHOUND AND P

Height e .

certainly he would not be so free from nervousness as if he frequented a menagerie where a reasonable range is given to the big cats. In the Roman wall-painting men carry very large shields, under which they quickly hide themselves when the lions approach. They are acting exactly like the tortoise which withdraws itself into the shell on the approach of a jaguar, but at least they can prevent the wild beast from turning their shelter over as the tortoise can not. A number of men provided with such shields were able, if we may trust the pictures, to gradually drive a wild beast into a trap, or to lasso or kill it if necessary. Evidently the Roman artist wished to show how the wild beasts were procured for the arena. Such a contrivance may be recommended to the sculptor who wishes to be yet more thorough than Barye and study great game, somewhat as one of the Parisian painters watches the life and landscape of the city from a cab.

But Barye was never so great a realist as certain artists of the present day. He had his realistic period, represented by the Tiger and Crocodile (1831) but the Lion and Serpent (1833) already shows a great change toward broader handling, while the Seated Lion shown in plaster in 1836 offers a proof that he was emancipated entirely from a petty way of looking at things. The management of the fur on this beast is strictly in sympathy with the grand modeling of the body as well as with that mighty look of aloofness in the lion which is so terrible yet fascinating to behold — a look that the sculptor has reproduced to a degree unknown to the present writer in any sculpture, ancient or modern.

IV

THE mistake of passing over Barye when great monuments for Paris were in question was perceived very generally about 1861. Though he was already past his prime, it needed another ten years to bring the public into sufficient movement to cause a demand for his services. If he had remained as vigorous and productive as during the years of abstention from the Salon, perhaps the neglect would have been continued; as he grew feebler and produced less, more attention was paid him. Barye recognized or perhaps imagined the falling off of his powers, for he remarked rather sadly to a friend who congratulated him on receiving a commission: 'I have waited all my life for patronage, and now it comes to me just as I am closing my shutters.' He realized that the most vigorous and productive years had been spent on small pieces which are certaidly wonderful enough, but must have seemed rather pitiable to an artist who felt himself equal to the largest and grandest efforts in his profession. It was a more than commonly hard example of *ars longa brevis vita*, for the art had been reached many years before it was demanded. One reason for this phenomenon rests on the longing for what one can not get. People looked about them and discovered that the whole half century had produced but one sculptor of animals who showed great genius.

Then, the reader suggests, of course commissions for animal groups came thick and fast!

Not at all. Barye was given a draped female Saint to carve in marble for a chapel in the Madeleine. In 1862 he received an order of an equestrian statue of Napoleon I in bronze to be erected at Ajaccio, Corsica, a spot he had never seen and indeed never did see, the monument being erected without his presence or care. The Sainte Clotilde at the Madeleine is sweet of face and graceful as to drapery but the Napoleon I at Ajaccio comes perilously near being a failure. Yet to the epoch 1850 to 1860 belong statues and groups into the making of which the best powers of Barye went. His merits as an artist risen from the ranks of artisans were never denied. Only he suffered from the caste feeling which introduced itself into such matters from the surrounding social atmosphere and which bade him remain an artisan and cease trying to be an artist.

We need not be surprised to find him in 1863 President of the Consultative Commission for what is called the Central Union of Arts applied to Industries. His statuettes were indeed conceived and modeled on a scale which adapted them to enlargement, but they were

No. 73.   WALKING LION IN SOLID SILVER.

Height, 13 Inches.

table and mantel ornaments nevertheless, even as Barye's enemies sneered. More strictly belonging to the field of arts applied to industries are the candelabra, such as those showing a stag rubbing its antlers against a trunk, or those designed on the poppy plant as the theme of ornamentation. In the Hôtel Pereire at Paris is a clock with a decoration by Barye never repeated and therefore unique. The figures of the Hours lead onward the horses of the Sun while Apollo himself guides the chariot. Separate studies for the chariot and female Hours together with a standing and a seated Apollo are in the ownership of his daughters.

Without ever becoming popular Barye had thus won for himself in his sixty-eighth year an enviable reputation as a sculptor and the warmest of friends as a lovable sturdy soul. When a piece of silver was needed for the Grand Prix at the Longchamps races Barye was asked to put in solid silver his Walking Lion, that august beast which shows in its gait as well as its face an anger colossal, yet as cold as befits a sovereign without ruth accustomed to destroy whatever comes in his path. This beautiful work which is now in Baltimore was won by Comte de la Grange with the racing mare Fille de l'Air.

A pretty story is connected with the piece which is fortunately not of the mythical kind. The sculptor had received a certain sum for the purpose, but on weighing the lion after casting, he discovered that there was less silver by weight in the object than he had received. To equalize matters and at the same time make it impossible for any charge against his honesty when all who knew the circumstances were dead, he cast some silver in flat bars and screwed them on the bottom of the stand without saying a word to anyone, thus bringing the whole up to the weight desired. This was only one case in point; he was always extremely sensitive of his personal honor and at times suffered in pocket more seriously than this in order to keep his self-respect untouched.

Eugène Delacroix died in this year, having fought his way into the Institute and having held aloof from Barye the greater part of his life.

In 1865 Barye was commissioned to model an equestrian statue of Napoleon I for the town of Grenoble. We have a statuette that embodies the sculptor's general idea; it is not very remarkable, though well-studied, and superior so far as regards the horse. Whilst he was at work on it in a studio hired for the purpose in the Rue Mouffletard he learned that M. Mercié had been asked to submit a model likewise. Instantly Barye decided to withdraw from the affair. But he would not do so in a vulgar way, by making a scene and by advancing the right of a sculptor of his eminence to a commission unbothered by a rival. He decided to give the authorities some civil excuse for throwing up the commission, and the letter which is reproduced here in fac-simile was the result. Observe that on this occasion when Barye would have been certain to explode with indignation, had he really been the hot-tempered, sharp-tongued man some anecdotes proclaim him, he is dignified, easy and even diplomatic. Some trouble with his landlord in the studio of Rue Mouffletard serves as the smoke under which he quietly leaves the field on the 16th of April 1866.

He was not without statues of human figures of the highest sort to prove his capacity, but unfortunately few knew of their existence. In 1854 the architect whose glory it is that he nearly finished the Louvre demanded from him a group in stone for one of the inner faces of the Carrousel court-yard—a group of War. M. Lefuel was so well pleased with War that he ordered three more groups on the spot, namely Peace, Order and Force. Strange to say these groups are seen by more people and can be better studied in the United States than in France. For while Lefuel perched them high up beyond the range of ordinary eye-sight, where they are overcrowded by the excessive ornamentation of the Louvre, the city of Baltimore has them on one of its open squares, just on a level with the eyes. The originals are of stone half the size of life, but they are rarely seen because impossible to examine properly without a scaffolding. The reproductions are in bronze and admirably adapted for examination. Perhaps they would be still better seen in Baltimore if placed near a wall, because the sculptor designed

NO. 74.

WAR.

Stone Group on Louvre.

NO. 75·

PEACE.

Stone Group on Louvre.

them with the intention of having their backs turned from the spectator. Their present arrangement at Baltimore has this advantage however that one can see how conscientiously Barye treated those parts of a group which were to remain unseen. There again we catch the Japanese touch—backs and insides must have their own thought bestowed on them, their own scheme of decoration.

It is certainly a marvel that Barye, after so long a neglect of his powers to model human figures for public monuments, should be able to work on them as if he were commonly asked for such things. Each group has an animal, a boy and a man, but each must be different from the other while preserving the same ideal of man and boy, and each must express a very generalized thought. War—peace—order—force: in these words there is no peg to hang a theme on. But the sculptor solves all four problems with an ease that makes one think of the Greek artists; the ease that contains no faintest suggestion of weariness, but on the contrary inexhaustible reserves of thought from which the artist may draw if so he wills. This effect, obscure though the points may be which cause the suggestion, is common to works of genius of all kinds.

Perhaps nothing distinguishes Barye more from the too clever artists which grew up in France before he died than a certain homely ruggedness about his groups of statuary which gives a false impression of the ease with which such things can be done. While some of the later brood of artists excite one at first by their marvelous dexterity of hand, they soon cease to interest. In sculpture the extreme of this is reached by those who indulge in tricks and prettinesses with marble that can not fail to extort surprise, but cause one presently an infinite weariness and disgust. Yet Barye did not go to the other extreme and neglect modeling out of anger and contempt for nigglers and literalists. He held his own road quietly without going from the line he thought best, either for the purpose of reforming sculpture or attempting to found a school. Yet found a school he did, little as he imagined himself doing anything of the kind. Perhaps all sculptors of animals must be to some extent his disciples, but we have in Mr. Edward Kemeys of New York a student of beasts who may go far if he takes to heart the life-giving conclusions that may be drawn from Barye's work and avoid external methods and the mere facile imitation of his subjects.

Of the four symbolical groups on the Louvre the first is unquestionably the finest. War, represented by a stalwart man laying his hand on a sword, a boy full of the thoughtlessness of extreme youth blowing gayly a trumpet, and by the horse, man's chosen comrade in war, has at once the alert and reposeful look befitting statuary of the best sort. In each group the animal is recumbent and forms the lower plane, being disposed in a semi-circle round man and boy. The horse of War with ears pricked looks out from the side of the seated man. In Force the lion holds much the same position; but what a different creature from that which marches so grimly, with such a scowl in the Walking Lion or looks with such sullen disdain from his pedestal near the Seine or wrinkles his horrid muzzle at the sight of the serpent! This is a sleepy lion lulled by the poppies of peace into that state of gentleness in which a child can drive it hither and thither. It may be that at the Jardin des Plantes the sculptor saw more than one lion reduced by age and captivity to the appearance of this type of strength.

Very different is the tiger in the group called Order. Here it typifies the perverse — the Communards, the Anarchists and the fishers in troubled waters. Forced to remain quiet, the sanguinary beast opens wide its mouth in a roar of rage. The bull in the group named Peace represents the peasantry and laboring classes generally, and the determined but quiet attitude of the man means that he typifies the force of good government, which protects labor. In all four the gestures are quiet though expressive enough. But they leave the impression that their maker is not a Frenchman; or if a Frenchman, then one of a previous age, say the comrade of Poussin who loved the classics and the classic land yet remained always a Gaul.

The foreign appearance of Barye's genius in his own land is a phenomenon that many may have noted but no one has explained. In the

NO. 76

ORDER.

Stone Group on Louvre.

NO. 77.

FORCE.

Stone Group on Louvre.

foregoing pages I have tried to lead back his peculiar characteristics to the scientific knowledge which he partly imbibed from the age, partly acquired by hard study. But there remains an element besides which may be likened to the instinctive qualities in contrast with the intellectual, the hereditary rather than the educated side of a person. Here we uncover one important root of Barye's personality. And whither does it lead? Not out of France, although it seems so foreign to our conventional ideas of a Frenchman as a gesticulatory and fickle man — brilliant but lacking in sturdiness.

Why not look for it in the lowest stratum of the populace, by which a bad stratum is not meant; the layer in fact which retains least mixed with their conquerors the populations that held France before the Kelts arrived? May we not refer such natures as Barye's, especially when we find them in solid figures like his, to the old populace of Europe, which was overspread by Kelt and Teuton until their language and religion became submerged and lost — the old folk of whom Finn and Esth and Magyar and Turk are living fragments? We have already seen that Barye's name may be explained to mean bear in these tongues and that from them English, German and Scandinavian obtain it, while Arkas and Arthur are its equivalents in the names meaning bear which are proper to the Aryan languages.

V

WHILST we are considering the four groups of the Carrousel Court it is proper to note that while in Peace the man, boy with flute and bull are at rest, so that they form an idyl in stone, and while Order is a group which is extremely reposeful with the exception of the tiger, the group of War and that of Force did not suggest to Barye violent movement. At the most War is energized by the uplifted elbow of the man whose hair is crowned with laurels and by the fine movement of the trumpet in the boy's hands. Yet even in the War group the horse merely raises its head and pricks its ears. Force is calmness itself, the lion as quiet as a purring cat, the little boy reflective as he props chin on hand, the man thoughtful and merely indicative of power through the magnificent muscles displayed by the arm that holds a stick. Among the four men of these groups assuredly he of Force is the subtlest as well as the nearest to the antique in his calm beauty. The boys are all charming, but perhaps the little fluteplayer winds his way deepest into one's affections. Among the four beasts it were hard to choose. They make one think of the emblems associated in the middle ages with three of the four Evangelists.

Those who study Barye carefully do not need these groups as witnesses to his consummate skill in modeling the human figure; for that skill was shown in embryo with the medal that won him a second prize in 1819. But for people who have investigated Barye no further than to realize his astonishing deserts as a sculptor of animals these groups will be a revelation. They must be placed by the imagination at a certain height against a background of architecture richly decorated, not half so high up however as the originals are, but about six or ten feet from the ground. Then the bent faces of the man and boy in three of the groups will be understood, as well as the peculiar symmetry of the grouping, which presents in each case the same general arrangement.

Naturally a criticism as to the place they ought to occupy in order to be seen to the best advantage holds good with the bronze copies, the only difference being that their apparent smaller size due to the dark color of the bronze demands for them a nearer view. Hence it might be well for Baltimore to ask that the bronzes on Mount Vernon Square be shifted from their present positions and placed against the base of the Washington Column in niches specially prepared for them. They would then get the proper altitude from which to be seen at their best and also the background similar to that which they have in the Louvre, but more advantageous in that it is simpler and will throw them into greater relief. Besides these four bronzes, Baltimore has, also through the liberality of Mr. Walters, a superb copy in bronze of the Lion in Repose that sits in duplicate by the river gate of the Louvre. This is also from the Barbédienne factory and likewise is of the same size as the original.

16 avril 1866

Monsieur

Le propriétaire de mon atelier de la rue Mouffetard m'ayant donné congé m'a mis dans l'impossibilité de commencer le grand travail de la statue équestre de l'empereur Napoléon I pour la ville de Grenoble. La conséquence de ce fait est de faire renoncer à l'exécution de ce travail. J'ai l'honneur de vous en prévenir.

Veuillez, Monsieur, agréer l'assurance de ma considération la plus distinguée.

Barye

NO. 79

AUTOGRAPH LETTER BY A L BARYE

Orders now began to flow in upon Barye. One of the legitimate glories of the reign of Napoleon III is the earnest effort made to advance the country in industries and the fine arts. The taste that presided at the Tuileries was far from faultless and many poor sculptors, painters and architects were favored; but some of the encouragements given with a generous hand fell to artists of the highest rank. Barye received a request for a model of an equestrian monument to Napoleon I in the town of Grenoble, but this as we have seen fell through because he became incensed that Mercié should have been asked also.

To 1866 belongs a bronze relief that was formerly to be seen on the Pavilion Lesdiguières over the entrance from the quay of the Seine into the same Carrousel Court of the Louvre. It was a triumphal scene in honor of Napoleon III who is depicted as a Roman conqueror. Napoleon III Dominating History and the Arts was one of Barye's failures, partly, it is said, because he was not allowed to carry it out in as high relief as he wished, but had to adjust his planes to the whims of others. It may be doubted whether he would have reached his own level in any case, for Napoleon III, whatever his virtues in seeking to foster the arts, was not the man to inspire an artist. Barye has made a delightful statuette of the Great Napoleon as Consul, where the Directoire uniform and the handsome young face lent themselves to art; but his monument for Grenoble which we have in a small bronze, and his monument at Ajaccio, Corsica, testify that the sculptor's originality became paralyzed when the problem was to model Napoleon as Emperor.

Barye was a man who spoke little and wrote not at all. To penetrate his thoughts we are forced back on his statuettes and other works of art. Judging from these one is tempted to conclude that he had no love or admiration for the ruthless Corsican and none for the dreamy nephew, under whose rule however he reached his greatest fame. Not a revolutionist by temperament, he was a man of the people and disliked autocrats. If a ruler was inevitable then he preferred a constitutional monarch of the type of Louis Philippe, to whose family, besides, he owed the first great encouragements and successes of his life.

But after all we can enter a very short way into the mind of a man like Barye. He belongs to the great classes on whose opinions the statesmen and politicians are forever speculating. Instead of talking they keep obstinately silent, and then, some fine day, discovering that things are not to their liking, rouse themselves and upset all the neat calculations of ambition and greed. All we can surely say of Barye is that his opinions have a certain guarded expression in the four groups that exist for the sparrows and pigeons on the Carrousel Court high up on the inner faces of Pavilions Denon and Mollien. As to Napoleon III Dominating History and the Arts it was saved from the fury of the mob in 1870 by a thick coat of plaster and was afterwards removed to the warehouses of the government, into which rejected articles are turned, as well as a thousand works of art purchased for one reason or another but never placed. Thence it has never emerged; no loss to the world therefrom !

The same spot that holds the four groups offers other examples of Barye's power to model the human nude in such a way as to preserve classical proportions yet gain the best decorative effect for architecture. That place over the arch leading to the Carrousel Court whence the equestrian bas-relief of Napoleon III was torn has river-gods, leaning each an arm on a jar. They are two youths differing one from the other in slight particulars. They are looking down as if at the water that is supposed to escape from the jar. They recall a lounging statue from the corner of a pediment on one of the most famous temples of Greece, but this is rather the result of the necessary adaptation of the human figure to a somewhat similar space than an imitation. The Greek sculptor had to put the legs of the figure into the narrow angle of the pediment. • Barye uses the somewhat triangular outline in order to gain the effect of supporters in heraldry; for the two river-gods were designed to flank that important slab on which Louis Napoleon figured as Julius Cæsar, his favorite model in history.

The rigid angles of Greek pediments are unbeautiful things, and the results to the sculptured figures introduced into them are, let us be

No. 78. THE SEINE: LEFT-HAND RIVER-GOD, LOUVRE.
Stone. Height, 38 inches.

frank about it, often most unfortunate. What can be worse than the
boxed and constricted look of some of the outer figures on the pediments of the Parthenon? In this case the pyramidal effect is produced, with a much more agreeable pitch to the slope, by the mass of
the figure itself. There is no harsh, stiff line impending over the
sculptures. It is heresy to attack the Greeks in anything, but their
merits will shine out all the more brilliant if their shortcomings are
not ignored. The wood-cut shows one of the two river-gods from
the reduction in bronze by M. Barbédienne.

But though Barye was at this time an old man and his merit as a
sculptor of the human figure was established by these handsome shapes,
it must not be supposed that he began to neglect the study of animals.
The more he worked at beasts the more problems arose and the deeper
grew his marveling at their beauty. The painter Fromentin passed the
greater part of his life struggling with the difficulties of the horse in
action, and his most candid biographer acknowledges that he never
succeeded in painting a horse as it can be done. Even Meissonier has
not completely mastered the action of the horse. When the instantaneous photograph was broached, he like many lesser lights fancied that
in such a means of certifying the actual position of the limbs during a
portion of a second we had found terra firma at last. Barye on the
other hand by virtue of genius united with intense application solved
the problem twenty times. In 1863 the American amateur who has
done him the greatest honors in our land called at his house on the
Quai des Célestins only to find that as usual he was not at home.
Madame Barye smiled in his earnest face and exclaimed:

'Ah, sir, there is no use calling for three weeks. *A new tiger has
arrived from Bengal; until its wildness is gone—no Monsieur Barye!*'

We have seen that Barye began the public exhibition of animal
groups with one that shows the greatest elaboration of hair, scales, folds
of skin, prominences and depressions of hide, even to trivial objects on
the fictitious ground where the struggle goes on. We have noted that
he very soon departed from this minute handling, showing more breadth

in Lion and Serpent, and still more in Seated Lion. This tendency toward omission of the unimportant is even seen in the little cat. It differs from ten thousand other seated cats wrought in terra-cotta, glass, porcelain, wood, ivory and stone, not to speak of metals, in that the modeling is very broad. Indeed when one first takes such a little object in hand the breadth irritates, for it looks like ignorance or carelessness. But try the experiment of having on your writing table a Barye cat and a seated cat by another artist, even an artist like Mêne who works in a broad way also, even a group by Cain. In the long run the uncarved, unworried handling of Barye tells and his statuette is preferred.

The same lesson is learned in painting. Here too the amateur begins by preferring canvases to which it is evident the painter has given many weeks of faithful toil. Perhaps it is one of those imitative things that charms the amateur, a painting of soiled currency or of placards pasted on a board fence, in which all kinds of tricks and illusions of the eye testify to the artist's cleverness of touch. Then this sort of painting palls and seems trivial. The next step is toward art of greater depth, but still obvious, logical, tangible art, if that word be permitted; say the paintings of Vibert and Gérome. But after passing through phases of admiration for Bouguereau and Meissonier, let us say, the amateur begins to long for something less obvious and more imaginative. He no longer asks that the painter tell everything. He is grateful to him if he do not, but will permit him, the amateur, to use his own powers of imagination to supply what is lacking, all the artist's strength going to the essentials, leaving the less important out. Here we have the amateur of paintings ready for symbolical and religious pictures of the best sort, and for landscapes like those of Corot and Rousseau, for landscapes with figures by Millet, and the works of those Impressionists of the present day who execute from original conviction and after profound studies, not because some other man has suggested that such handling pays at least in the coin of notoriety, if in no other.

This is a summary sketch of the development that has gone on in the taste of a thousand collectors in France and the United States. Many

NO. 11.

SEATED CAT

Height 4½ inches

of them protested at every step an indifference, if not abhorrence, of
the works of art they were soon to take to their hearts; but the march
of understanding was too strong for them. Coming to curse, they
remained to pray. The very men who were once outspoken in their
irritation because of an apparent slovenliness of work have been found,
a few years after, giving large prices for exactly the same sort of products they formerly denounced.

This little comedy of the amateur regarded as a genus goes on constantly and rewards the critic for a great deal that is distasteful in his
pursuit. For those artists who have been abandoned there is always
one consolation. In an alert community like ours, where the average
culture is at a pretty high level, there is a constant supply of recruits
who are fitted exactly to understand and enjoy the work of each artist.
Many collectors hold to their early admirations, while for each one
of those who desert their former loves ten patrons spring up in the
stratum of intelligence for which the artist is able to cater.

Barye, it may surprise a good many persons to learn, was an impressionist in his own way, and at times as extreme an impressionist as ever
Mr. Whistler in etching or M. Monet in paint. He was an impressionist
more after the order of Courbet however. A bronze that is included
by Barbédienne in his Barye reproductions for commerce was taken
from a model that Barye cherished. It was a lion seated, differing from
the Lion of the Louvre gate, and from two or three small bronze seated
lions. It is so unwrought, so composed of masses rather than curves
that it recalls the unfinished marbles by Michael Angelo one sees in
Florence. It was very natural that a visitor, seeing this in Barye's
studio, should ask when he meant to finish it.

' It is finished enough for me ' replied the sculptor.

We need not suppose that Barye would ever have given this lion to
the world, as M. Barbédienne has. It is well enough, now that he has
a host of admirers, to offer them an example in bronze of a model at the
point where it pleased the sculptor to rest content and give not one
stroke more. But had Barye issued it there would have been the fewest

possible buyers and the sculptor would have been accused of affectation. It is now an interesting example to place in large collections of these bronzes and is merely noted in connection with what has gone before concerning that evolution of taste which becomes impatient of the unimportant and longs merely for the suggestion from which to evolve a thought. The reader will easily recall exactly parallel movements in the development of taste in literature and music; but such an excursus would lead too far away from the province of this book.

The year 1866 was for Barye one in which the bitter-sweet might have been his symbol. There appeared in L'Illustration an article by Théophile Gautier, that old lion of Bohemian Paris, with a portrait on wood engraved by Mouilleron. But the bitter must have been peculiarly like gall to a man of Barye's temperament. His friends induced him to offer himself for election to the Institute of France and he was rejected. What inducements they made to bring him to the necessary visits one would like to know. But those who study Barye through these acts as well as his products in art will hardly need to be told that such a step indicated a consciousness on his part that his career as an original genius was over, and that for the sake of his wife and children he ought to neglect nothing that would better their prospects, even at the expense of his lifelong pride. If he died 'of the Institute' there was a pension. Besides, his bronzes, water-colors and the rest would naturally fetch higher prices as the work of a member of the Institute.

Barye had little reason to respect the opinion on art matters of any large body of persons, whether artists or literary men. He had not been like many of his comrades of 1830 a violent abuser of the clever writers and nonentities who gained a place in the Institute, but under his firmly closed lips it was not hard to detect a foe to such distinctions. Now he bowed to prejudice and for the sake of his family put the cup to his lips. It was the cup of humiliation — but even so he was not permitted to enjoy it.

Some balm awaited his pride the next year however for he gained the Grand Gold Medal for bronzes. He was a member of the jury for the

Exposition and while serving his likeness was caught one day in a pen and ink sketch by the sculptor Carpeaux whose works, while in nowise imitative of Barye's, show the salutary influence the latter exerted on sculpture generally by entering a protest against trivial, niggling work. It has been hinted that Barye would have derived much more benefit financially speaking, had he received the First Gold Medal for his bronzes, owing to the power that medal has in advertising wares to which it has been awarded. By suggesting to the authorities that an extraordinary honor should be awarded Barye the practical bronze founders are said to have done a clever stroke of business for themselves and flattered the sculptor at the expense of his pocket. However that may be — and he was certainly exposed to similar intrigues more than once in his career as a tradesman — the medal was a distinguished mark of honor.

The same year (February 1867) an article on him appeared in the Gazette des Beaux Arts from the accomplished pen of M. Paul Mantz which doubtless contributed not a little to spread an understanding of the man, his methods and aims. So recently as May 1889 the Gazette opened its pages to the painter Bonnat, a lifelong admirer of Barye. He has given us an enthusiastic note on the master which will take rank beside the portrait he painted of him after death, a reproduction of which will be found among these illustrations.

It should be noted however that the very remarkable group belonging to M. Bonnat which is pictured for that article is misnamed *Aurochs Attaqué par un Serpent.* The beast wrapped in the folds of the python snake is a gnu, that singular combination of horse, antelope and ox, which is found in Africa whère the great snakes also exist. The aurochs is practically extinct, and when it did live was a denizen of climates too cold for the python. The gnu has a certain resemblance to the musk-ox of the Arctic Circle; whence in all probability the mistake arose.

About this period of his life he received an order from Marseilles which must have pleased him, because it showed that somebody besides

Americans noted his power. The Chateau d' Eau is a fine building in a classic style which ornaments the reservoirs that supply the city with water. To adorn this building four colossal groups in stone were ordered, namely: one-sided combats between tigers and a stag and a doe, and two other groups in which the lion is the aggressor, the prey being in one case a boar, in the other an antelope. These colossi were thought so well of that plaster casts of them were afterwards shown in Paris at the Exposition.

With the year 1868 the crowning glory so far as the public is concerned reached Barye in his election to the Institute. How it came about is not easy to ascertain, but the story current was that the architect Lefuel, a great friend of the sculptor, took him driving one day, and stopping at a house persuaded Barye to come in with him. On entering the latter found himself visiting one of the Immortals and the secret was out. His friend, knowing that after his rejection in 1866 nothing would induce Barye to make the obligatory round of calls on the men who held the chairs, had brought him to the point by strategy. Once in the distasteful round, Barye persevered and was duly elected. With this closed what may be called his active career as an artist. He had already shown the defection of his powers in the relief of Napoleon III as a Roman in triumph. Now indeed the time had come when, in his homely bourgeois phrase, it was time to put up the shutters.

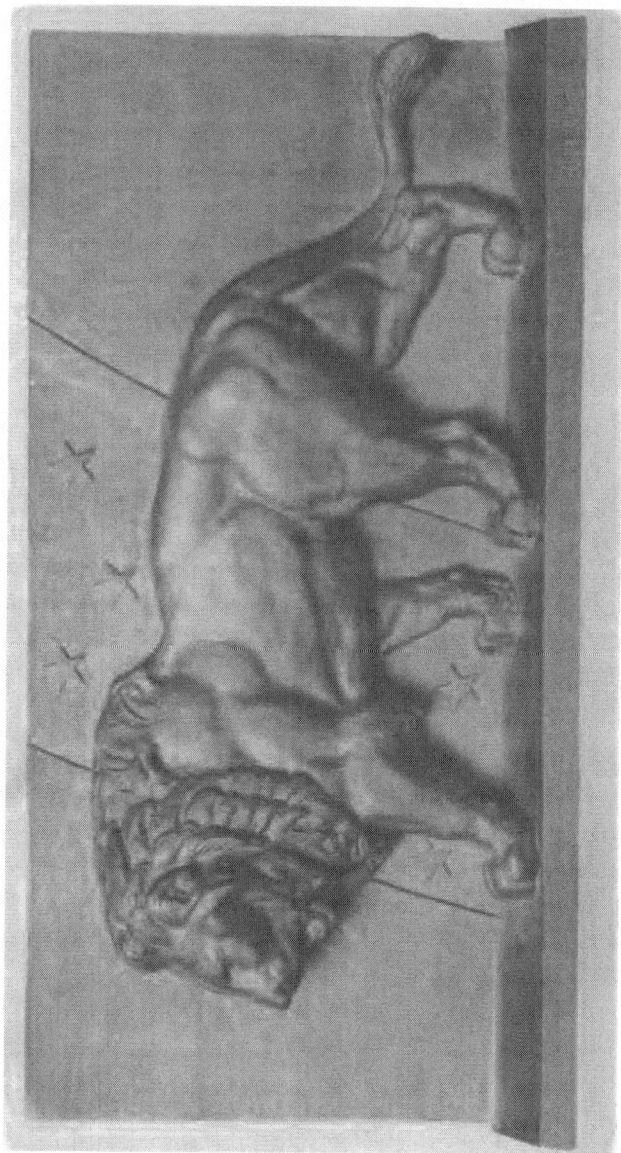

NO. 51.

LION OF THE JULY COLUMN PLACE BASTILLE

Reduction 8½ inches high

Chapter Five

I

THE artist, the author, the soldier ought to perform a supreme act of creation or of courage and pass away while the world that can understand is still ringing with the achievement. But those sturdy natures in whom a physical power is the comrade of an intellectual are often and one may say commonly destined to outlive their period of high achievement.

This was the case of Barye. He survived the creative epoch about twenty years, since we may consider the four groups for the Cour du Carrousel the terminus of his career as a sculptor. Some of his latter-day works fell below his mark. They are not weak, for it seems impossible that Barye should be weak. But they are commonplace, but they are dull. How much this had to do with old age, how much with an uncongenial subject is not readily seen. Either or both. It would have been beyond human likelihood that he should have made a success in every case, given the great quantity and range of his work, extending as it does from the cold blooded reptiles with skeletons on the exterior of their frames to the higher mammals both herb-eating and flesh-eating, to the anthropoid apes and to the human being. Nay, not content with this range, Barye essayed the monsters, embodying what we learn of their shapes from the literatures of Assyria, Greece and Rome. Even this could not serve as his limit, for he dared to vie with the inimitable masters of the past and model the portraits of goddesses and of saints.

But not to mention his failures would be unfair. The worst of all was that relief in the Roman spirit representing Louis Napoleon as a patron of the arts. There was something cruel in asking a sculptor of Barye's antecedents to do such a work, and perhaps there was malice in the commission; for his friends had been loud in their blame of the neglect with which he was treated. Yet after all it may have been sheer bureaucratic stupidity. A connoisseur needed to review but a little of Barye's career to know that he was strongest in symbolical and mythological subjects into which animal figures enter. What a magnificent Roc carrying off Sinbad the Sailor would not Barye have created! How he would have reveled in the symbols of the Four Evangelists, giving to eagle, steer, lion, ay and angel the touch of the supernatural, of which he almost alone in this century possessed the secret! He alone could have modeled a Pegasus that had all the power of the horse and the buoyant look of the bird. With one hint from a certain Greek coin he might have designed a sea-serpent which would satisfy the most skeptical that such a creature, if it existed at all, must have had just that form. But as luck would have it, the only piece of work by Barye very prominent in Paris, one that could not be evaded on approaching the Louvre by the quay along the Seine, was that very relief of Napoleon III trying to be Julius Cæsar which represents the lowest ebb of Barye as an artist! Fortunately it has not troubled the admirers of the sculptor since 1870.

When the day of disillusionment came and the French found themselves without armies or Emperor, the latter became the scapegoat and no portrait of him was safe. Cowards and blusterers who dare not face the bullet are always ready to lead in deadly assaults upon pictures and statues. But the bas-relief, which really deserved to suffer from the iconoclast, was not permitted to be ruined. Some mistaken friend covered it with a thick layer of plaster to prevent its destruction at the hands of rascals. The republic respected it so far as to relegate it to some warehouse, but at the time of the exhibition of Barye's works this spring it could not be found.

By 1873 Barye was so conscious of the loss of his powers that he declined an order for a vase given him under the most liberal and flattering terms. Not that he was enfeebled and could not work. He was still an active old man. But he knew that he could not produce as in former years. The vase was to have combats of Lapiths and centaurs in relief, so that he did not need to study fresh kinds of figures. There were the sketches for the great group of 1850. But where another might have done his best and pocketed the commission, relying on the fame he had already won, Barye felt scruples.

There was another reason for declining this commission. He was occupied by a task that must have been extremely gratifying to a man who, on looking back through almost the whole of the century, could not feel that he had been treated by his country according to his deserts. Mr. Corcoran of Washington having great confidence in the taste of Mr. Wm. T. Walters, and wishing to have the benefit of that taste in fitting with works of art the superb building which is now a monument to his memory, made him chairman of the committee to select exhibits. In that capacity Mr. Walters called on Barye in 1873 and after a pleasant conversation remarked:

'Monsieur Barye, I come to make you a proposition. I come to commission you to supply the Corcoran Gallery at Washington with one specimen of every bronze you have designed throughout your life.'

This speech, remarked Mr. Walters, to whom I am indebted for the anecdote, produced the liveliest effect on the staid countenance of Barye. His eyes filled with tears and he spoke with difficulty:

'Ah, Monsieur Walters! My own country has never done anything like that for me!'

So it was that the Corcoran Gallery at one time possessed the fullest collection of bronzes by the master in America and probably in the world, though many of the smaller pieces have been lost since then by theft, from which the custodians of the gallery could not protect objects that could be slipped into a good-sized pocket. The losses in this way became so serious that holes were drilled in the metal stands of the figures and they were bolted to the shelves on which they were displayed. But even so the passion for owning a bronze, though pilfered, was so great that they were sometimes wrenched from the shelf and carried off. The most singular and discreditable part of this is, that the thieves were persons of outward respectability who did not steal from poverty, or to sell the bronze again, but from a desire to own it. They were intelligent and up to a certain point cultivated persons, perhaps in some instances afflicted with hereditary thievishness which in the case of respectable persons is dignified with a Greek name and called kleptomania. Barye's bronzes, in fact, were as difficult to keep as the rare old books which have tempted scholars from the straight road.

Barye set himself to do justice to this magnificent commission before the weakness of old age overtook him, for he was then already seventy-seven. He managed to send to the Corcoran Gallery no less than one hundred and twenty bronzes before the grim spectre which he had suggested so many times in his conflicts of animals and men came to his bedside and bade him submit to the inexorable law of which he had been the curious and sombre poet.

About this time, whilst he was confined to the house by an illness, his wife essayed to interest him by chatting about his works as she dusted the bronzes in the little workshop. ' You should cut the names on these groups clearer' she remarked ' when you feel better.'

Barye lifted his head from his hand and said :

' Within twenty years, my dear, people will be studying my signature with a magnifying glass.'

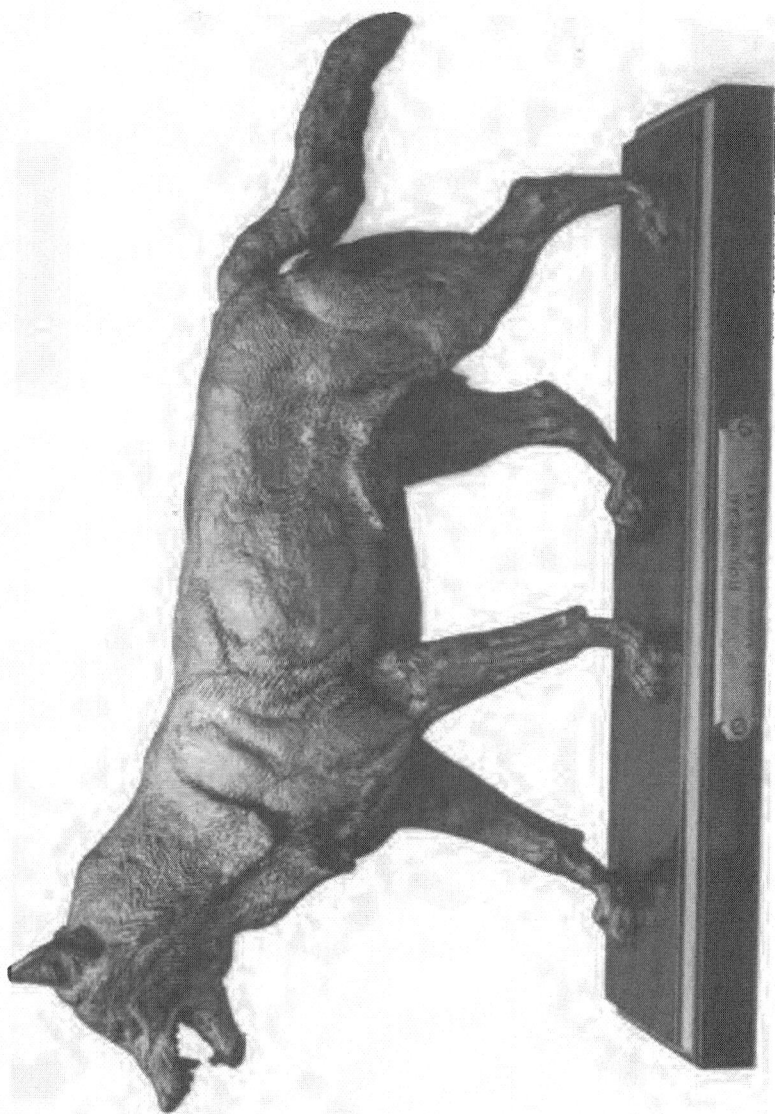

NO. 80.

GROWLING WOLF WALKING (R. BEUTAU'S)

Height 8½ inches

II

ONE by one his friends had been falling, and in 1875 the sculptor found that little band in Barbizon strangely shrunk. Corot was about to die, and Millet was ill. Rousseau, for whom he had finished with loving care a wonderful specimen of the Growling Wolf which is now in the Walters collection, labelling it 'À l'Ami Rousseau, Son Admirateur A. L. Barye'—the great landscape painter Rousseau had brought his uneventful yet tragic life to a close twelve years before. Like him Barye was a Parisian who rarely left Paris and never France. Like Corot he suffered years of eclipse only to be hailed at the end of his life as in certain lines the greatest artist ever produced by France. Like Millet he was the unobtrusive silent champion of a race, not of men, but of the dumb animals which have suffered tortures beyond the estimate of man's brain because man has kept them too low and far away from himself. And, like Millet also, he found the United States full of admirers. Like Diaz again he was a colorist though he wrought in patinas, whether frosted with silver like that on the Growling Wolf, or red as copper like that on the Asian Elephant Walking, or lovely olive green such as one sees on some of the Walking Tigers or the Panther Pulling Down a Stag. For these men the year 1875 was fateful, as if they could survive no longer the disasters of 1870 which had cut so deeply into the souls of some of them, notably of Millet. In June there was no hope, and on the afternoon of the 25th Barye breathed his last.

Although his reputation, waxing with his honors and the decline of his creative ability, brought more ease to his latter years, Barye died a poor man, a much poorer man for instance than Millet. He had two daughters by his first wife. Portraits of them exist in Paris and are among the happiest of his works in water-colors. By his second wife he had eight children, and as it seems fated that in so large a family there must always be black sheep, so in Barye's there was one who tried cruelly the kindness of the sculptor.

To utter bronzes with the name of the artist affixed is a kind of forgery much worse in its effects than the ordinary forgery of a check, because it makes very nervous the buyers who learn of the fact that such bronzes exist. Barye was indeed pursued through life by imitators and falsifiers who knew much better than he the art of selling. Whilst he lived there were men base enough to issue bronzes from models by him which they secured in one way or another, sometimes through sales at critical moments of Barye's financial career, sometimes by thoroughly illegal means. Wretched copies were at one time sold in New York but the demand was too small from the ignorant and the connoisseurs knew their Paris too well to be taken in very often.

Yet it is not in the past alone that danger existed. Ungenuine Barye bronzes, in the sense that they are offered as works which passed his own stern censorship, yet are in fact modern casts, can be found in more than one place in Paris. Sometimes the seller is honestly taken in himself, or he is truthful enough to acknowledge that the bronze is new but taken from a genuine model once in Barye's shop. But without the advice of an expert like Mr. Lucas of Paris it is unwise to buy Barye 'old bronzes' in France at present. Better invest in the Barbédienne reproductions of which especially the earlier pieces are excellent up to a certain point and reasonable in price.

Barye died too early to feel the gratification of knowing that five of his finest works had been erected in a city by the sea far across the Atlantic. But he did know that Americans were the most appreciative and steady customers for his smaller bronzes and he had the pleasure of watching the growth of at least two great collections of such of his works as were not too bulky for convenient shipment, namely the Corcoran Gallery in Washington and that of Mr. Walters in Baltimore. He knew also that a number of gentlemen of New York and Boston were gathering collections of his bronzes and water-colors. Yet he died poor in a small dingy house on the Quai des Célestins where the statuettes were by no means confined to the little shop in the front room, but pervaded more or less the whole house.

NO. 55.

MEDIÆVAL PEASANT (FROM BÄR HUND)

Height 12 inches

III

IN France a certain ceremony at funerals is obligatory, however humble a man's circumstances may be, provided the dead was of the Legion of Honor. In this ornamental fraternity Barye was an officer and his funeral was therefore graced by an escort of soldiers. He was also a member of the Institute and had been a Professor at the Jardin des Plantes. The École des Beaux Arts was likewise represented and several foreign admirers of Barye, hearing of the ceremony, among them Mr. S. P. Avery of New York, were sufficiently interested to form part of the procession.

At the house some very distinguished artists made their appearance, such as Meissonier, Gérome, Carolus Duran and Bonnat, and were not backward in praise of the sculptor whose worth each one knew well. Was not Bonnat the owner of various groups by Barye? And did not Gérome come to the sculptor for a lion fit to stand in the arena of Rome? But these might have come to the funeral of any distinguished artist of their acquaintance. There were other mourners on the Quai des Célestins that day.

The French workingman was there in his blouse, but in scattered groups. He did not make his appearance in force until the march to the grave was taken up. Then the blouses began to issue from workshops and factories until it was plain to the world that somebody more than commonly dear to the artisan world of Paris was passing to his last rest. The artists conducted Barye but the artisans followed. They knew that in him the highest rank of the artistic career had been entered by way of the jeweler's bench and the foundry. It is more than likely they knew that his unaided genius had conquered a place for him in two worlds which are not always of the same opinion; namely in the highest world of society as well as that of the artists. For they could not but remember that Barye had the privilege of knowing intimately the Duke of Orleans, whose unlikeness to his father Louis Philippe, whose soldierly, generous nature and especially whose untimely death before he had a chance to rule, idealized his memory in their thought. They knew of course that Barye was well thought of under the Napoleonic revival of 1852. But they were also certain that as in the origin he had sprung from the people, so to the last he had remained a people's, without ever becoming a popular, man. His head had never been turned by honors and favors from the great. Always under his somewhat melancholy and reserved manner was felt the sturdy manhood of a character that knew its limits and its path.

In October of 1875 there was an exhibition of Barye bronzes and water-colors at the École des Beaux Arts, and people who went there out of curiosity were astonished at the fecundity of Barye's genius, not to speak of the quantity of works, completed and incomplete, in bronze, terra-cotta, plaster, stone, oils, water-colors and crayon. Three equestrian statuettes in wax were shown which did not make a reappearance at the exhibition this spring at the École des Beaux Arts, viz: St. George and the Dragon, La Renommée, and Julius Cæsar. There were also the plaster cast touched with wax of a Python Crushing a Gnu as well as a Nereid Arranging Her Necklace, a bronze now in the possession of Monsieur Vial. Among the other objects was a *guépard*, or small wild-cat of India (*Felis jubata*) and a Chimæra in wax, now owned by Monsieur Vial.

There also appeared the dreadful little group which may be seen in the artotype, a Horseman of Africa Surprised by a Python, in the plaster model touched up with wax. This is now in Monsieur Barbédienne's large collection of Barye objects. A detail of some importance is not shown in the illustration to account for the position of the horse. The snake has taken a loop round the stump of a tree and crushes horse and horseman against the stump on the other side of the group. The attack has been so sudden that the horseman is seized by the throat before he can either slip from the saddle or use his weapons. The scene is one that appeals to every age. Although the books in which such

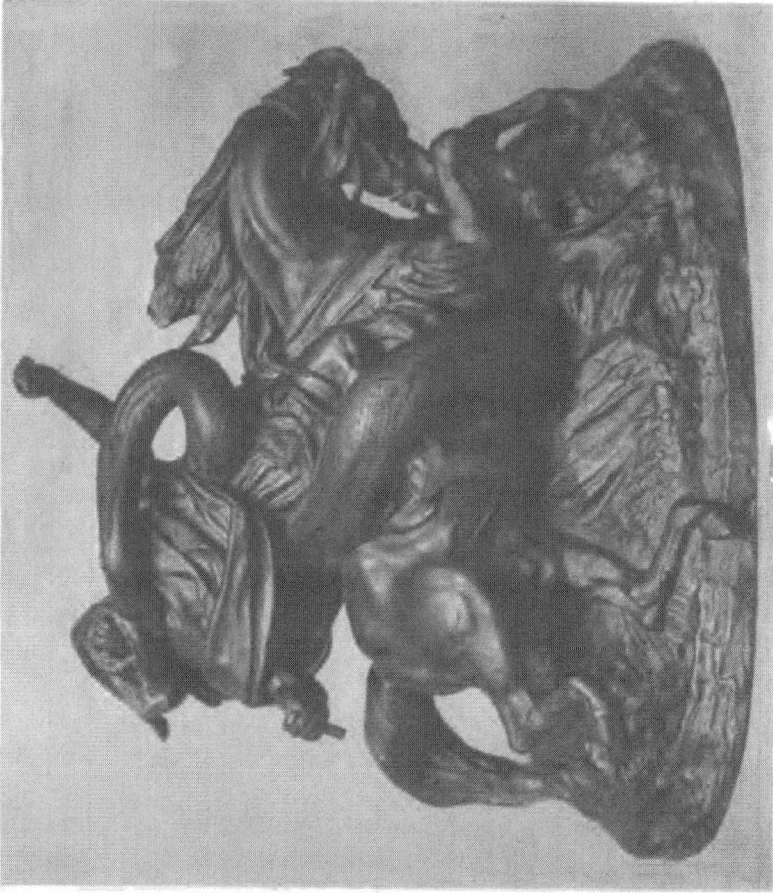

NO. 69

PYTHON CRUSHING AFRICAN HORSEMAN

Height 8½ inches

adventures are told are now prepared chiefly for boys, who have the hunger for curious animals and strange adventures with beasts that adults are supposed to outgrow, yet it may be safely said that no one can regard this battle without some emotion, even if it be one of unmitigated horror. Who shall blame the person who turns away from it with a shudder? The man who could model such terrible things had in him the quality that made Dante while still in life an object of no little terror to the populace. It is to such groups as this that we may turn in order to account for the various stories regarding Barye which give the impression that his was a morose and forbidding nature.

Among the articles left by Barye in his studio were plaster models for the four great beast conflicts in stone at the Chateau d'Eau in Marseilles. A sketch in terra cotta of a Bear Overthrowing a Buck (fallow deer) is now in the possession of Mr. Deloye who also owns a terra cotta sketch of a Jaguar Overthrowing an Antelope. These were Barye's first ideas for the groups at Marseilles, but he concluded in the end to have two lions and two tigers with different hoofed animals for their prey. Mr. Theodore Kane Gibbs perhaps has the Jaguar Overthrowing an Antelope, carved half the size of life in a very hard stone. Mr. J. F. Sutton has a large bronze of this same group and the Walters Gallery another produced by the galvano-plastic process. The stone group appears to have been made between 1868 and 1875, the period in which Barye fashioned in hard stone for the Comte de Nicolaï his favorite greyhound Tom.

An article in the Gazette des Beaux Arts by Monsieur Genevay was the beginning of that movement for a monument to Barye of which this work is part. It was most appreciative and made readers aware of the loss France suffered in the death of this quiet and unpretentious statuary. The exhibition was followed by a sale at the Hôtel Drouot which surprised everyone, not at all because of the high prices that were paid but of the apathy of the public. Barye when living was patronized by comparatively few people; when dead he did not enjoy that sudden popularity among the buyers of art objects and bric-à-brac which often comes like a smile of irony to close the career of much smaller men. So indifferent was the public that it was almost like a charity when M. Barbédienne bought in the greater part of his models and rarer pieces, although it must have been plain enough that such works could be made immensely profitable with time in experienced hands, a forecast that has been abundantly justified since. The reason for this apathy is worth a little consideration.

IV

AT the opening of Barye's career I reviewed some of the obstacles that rose before him on the way he trod, obstacles that had their origin in religious ideas, obstacles springing from imperfect knowledge of the earth and its inhabitants whether human or bestial. During the half century that lies between 1825 and 1875 many of these stumbling-blocks were removed by the progress of science, and Barye himself did something to affect the same result. In his own field, by his own studies, which were indeed based on science but did not appeal obviously to scientific minds nor indeed suggest science to those who were influenced by his creations, he helped men to a wider and fairer view of animated beings on earth, seizing this one on the side of simple curiosity, that one through his faculty of perceiving a beauty in unusual things not commonly treated in the arts, and a third by the mere technical excellence of his touch as a modeler and bronze founder.

But a statue or group admired when of large size and in the open air may not please so much if it be a statuette that holds its place on the mantel-board or the writing-desk. In the home the subjects that seem most appropriate are gentle figures in oils, water-colors, marble, ivory or bronze which do not suggest thoughts of bloodshed and cruelty. Children might perhaps learn to be cruel, many a parent has thought, if they saw constantly before their eyes combats and carnage, even if only between wild beasts. The sports of the arena in Rome, the bull-fights of Spain, the bear-baitings of our immediate ancestors of northern

122

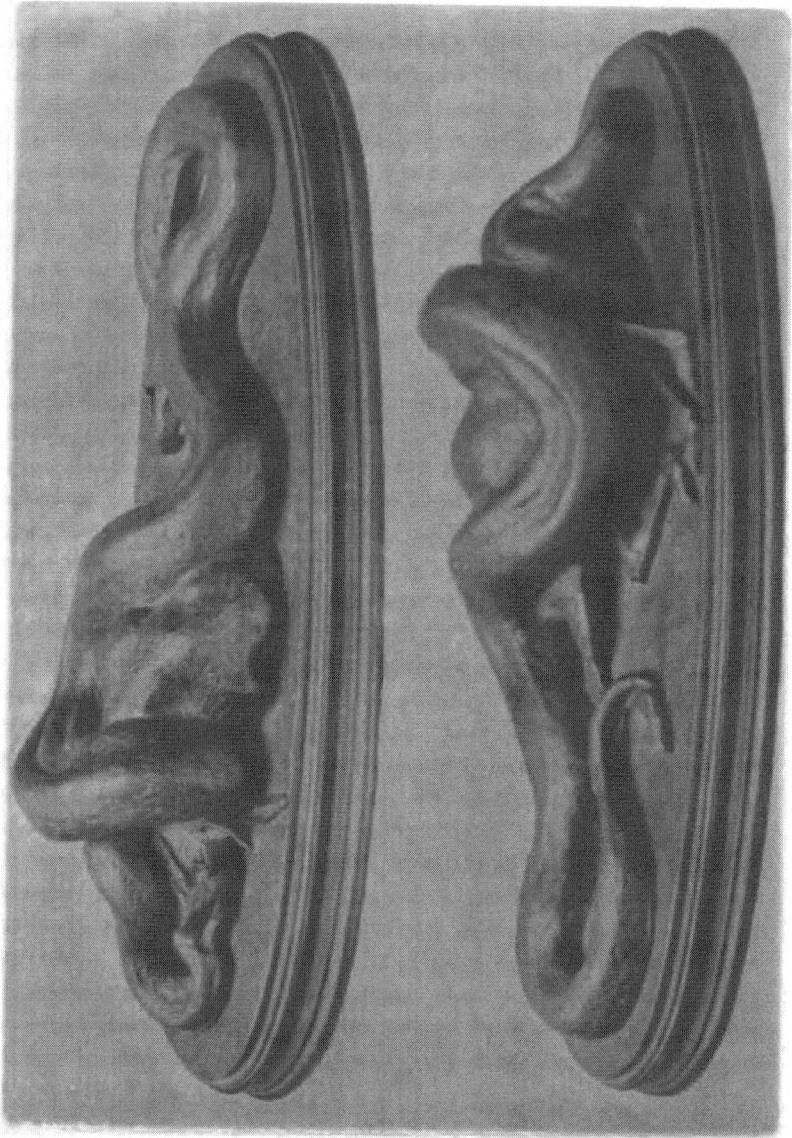

Europe are supposed to have been a harm to public morals by accustoming the people from infancy to the idea of bloodshed.

Now the illustrations in this book are enough to show what a procession of frightful shapes passed beneath the quiet strong hands of Antoine Louis Barye during that half-century so recently elapsed! Many a man who knew well how beautiful his bronzes were must have hesitated before bringing them into his home, fearing lest his children might acquire some uncanny taste for blood by seeing these tigers devouring the innocent croppers of the grass, elephants transfixing tigers with their tusks, pythons crunching life and shape out of crocodiles, or jaguars gloating over their newly-slain prey. Nay, he may have feared that the child unborn might suffer irretrievable harm through the eyes of its mother if there should be any substratum of fact in the fancies on that head which the ancients believed in all their fullness and the moderns themselves are slow to class among superstitions. Granted therefore that the present age has become too enlightened to oppose the making of such sanguinary works of art, there remains the practical certainty with respect to a large body of men capable of enjoying the marvelous genius of Barye that his bronzes were in large part banished their homes.

But when I say men I am only speaking of not quite half the community of those whose wealth and education permit them to acquire luxuries like bronzes of this kind. The larger half of that community consists of women. It will hardly be denied that there is need of much more cultivation in the fine arts, more study and reading, on the part of a woman to fit her to appreciate the terrible groups by Barye than are necessary to a man. She has to overcome, besides her greater sensitiveness to the horrible, her naturally stronger repugnance to scenes of death. Man is the physically stronger person in whom the instinct of battle is bred. The sight of a dog-fight or cock-fight is not pleasing to women, but the best of men must have felt, perhaps with a touch of shame, that such a scene awakes their curiosity to see which will win—who knows? stirs an obscure feeling, a glow, a longing to be of the battle!

When therefore a man admires combats modeled by Barye it does not follow that woman must. On the contrary the chances are that the average woman who screams if she sees an innocent little snake the length of her arm will feel the most violent aversion to such works of art. And she will be just as right and normal in so doing as the man is when he experiences a certain glow of pleasure at a sight that makes her shudder.

Here is the place to call attention to a singular fact which rarely escapes the person who examines the old catalogues of Barye and reviews large collections of his bronzes. Along with Barye's strongly masculine nature (if it be masculine to be stern, reserved and silent, to suffer without murmuring and pursue steadfastly an aim across all obstacles) along with a nature that at least can hardly be called feminine, went a predilection for the male in all his statuary. This was most obvious in his animal groups. He modeled, it is true, hinds and does. Along with a little bronze of a moufflon ram goes an ewe. There are two small statuettes of lionesses walking which vary slightly in the shape of their heads and ears. But these are exceptions to the grand rule that consciously or unconsciously Barye modeled the male in preference to the female, and so consistently did he do this throughout his life that it seems intentional. How otherwise did he escape from the mare and the cow, the ewe of the common sheep and the females of various breeds of dogs which offer considerable differences from their males in shape, size and disposition of coat?

And yet when he did model the female he was not weak or indifferent. The lionesses just mentioned are superb pieces notwithstanding their little size, having to the full that look of haughty and lonely grandeur which is found in the lion. But his figures of women are still more remarkable for their beauty. While they are few compared with the figures of men, they have a certain grandeur. The equestrian statuette called L'Amazone, a lady in the riding costume of 1830 or thereabouts, is a marvel of balance. She sits her horse magnificently. None of the painters of that period who have tried their hand at the same

124

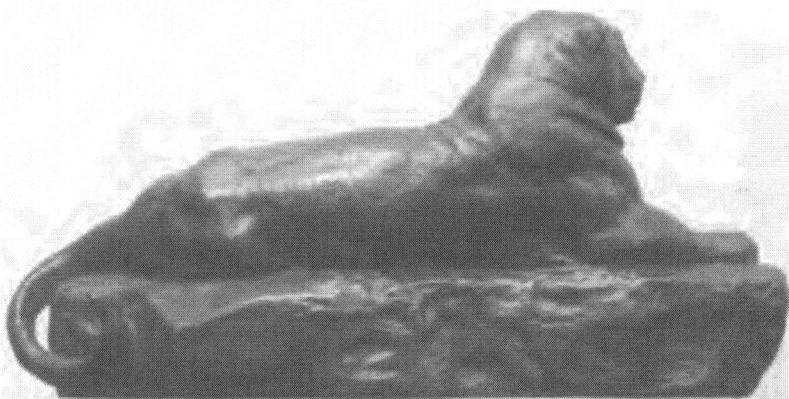

NO. 39.

PANTHER OF TUN'S COUCHANT

Height 3¾ inches

subject approach Barye either as regards the horse or with respect to the lady's seat in her saddle. The Angelica on the Hippogriff, the three goddesses and three Graces on the candelabra belonging to that group and the figures of the Hours on the great clock at the Hôtel Pereire testify how firmly and powerfully, yet with what delicacy Barye could mold an image in the form of woman. This however makes it all the more odd that he should have employed his talents so rarely in fashioning the female of men and beasts.

V

As a matter of fact when he died Barye had not made a conquest of the more important half of the persons to whom he might look for appreciation and patronage. The size of his works fits them for the adornment of the house. The husband who admired a Barye bronze of conflict between animals could not very well introduce it into the home against the swift condemnation of the wife. Those who did had to support the constant protest of their spouses. In the end the woman was likely to win and cause the banishment of the piece to the garret or the bric-à-brac shop. The curious difference on the subject of these groups by no means ended soon after Barye's death when he became even more famous than during life. It did not end then, and has not ended now.

In all probability it never will end. Each year the circle of women whose knowledge of art and wider education permits them to overcome their inborn dislike of such things increases. Each year more women as well as men learn to distinguish the art of a given work from the bald fact it happens to set forth. But it is too much to expect that such instincts as the hatred of the feminine half of humanity for works of arts that suggest dreadful scenes from which they would fly if they saw them realized will ever be sufficiently overborne by the artistic merits of such objects to make them love and cherish Barye's bronzes of conflict. Perhaps it is better they should not. What can be more disillusioning than to see a beautiful Spaniard applauding the sickening sights of a bull-fight? And yet it must be conceded that these very women who look on unconcerned when a horse is gored make good mothers, sisters and wives.

But the digression has taken us far from the event in question, the sale of Barye's works at the Hôtel Drouot in 1875. It accounts for the lack of popularity of his bronzes which, by no fault of his own but of his countrymen in power, were of a size that fitted them only for interiors, whereas they should have been prepared for great monuments. His life proper ends with this sale, for then the great bulk of his studio properties, models in bronze, wax, terra-cotta and plaster, his oils, water-colors and drawings were dispersed and his fame then entered on another phase, one that was wider and more soundly based and one of which the eventual limits are hard to determine.

One may ask what would have been the present state of Barye's fame, had Americans never interested themselves in his works and brought the wider circle of French amateurs and dealers in objects of art to a realization of his worth. It may well be questioned whether the small and devoted band in France who were the first to appreciate Barye and trumpet his praises could ever have overcome the dead weight of popular indifference had they not been assisted from the other side of the Atlantic.

For many years it was supposed in France that anything was good enough for Americans and in consequence of that supposition it was believed that painters and some few sculptors got rid of their inferior wares to rich citizens of the United States. One fine day somebody had the hardihood to remark that the Yankees were not so stupid as they seemed and were even taking away masterpieces. The statement was scoffed at for a while, until one writer after another corroborated the report, and some even made use of intemperate language as is the wont of certain Parisian journalists when foreigners are concerned, taking Americans to task for draining France of the finest canvases of the times.

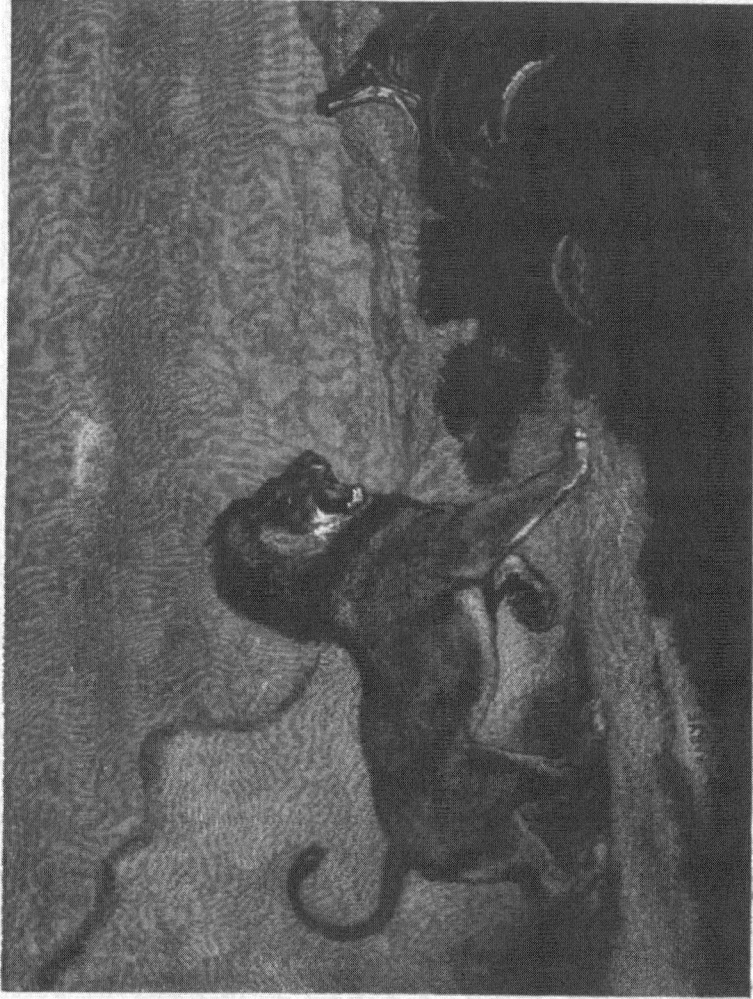

No. 33. LION MEETING PYTHON SNAKE (water-color).

11¼ x 18¾ inches.

However one may smile at the folly of imputing in Americans such a compliment to the French as a crime, the fact remains that the large prices for bronzes by Barye and paintings by Delacroix, Millet, Rousseau, Corot and others of the Barbizon school, have had a powerful effect in France. They have increased the average Frenchman's respect for his own artists and caused him to pay gladly such prices for works formerly neglected as he never would have believed possible. An extreme instance was the price Monsieur Proust wished to pay for the Angélus by Millet at the sale of M. Secrétan's gallery; another was the great price the government did pay for the Deer Covert by Courbet. If it be true that Americans have 'ruined the market', to adopt the language of the trade in art objects, it is equally true that only since the French have been forced to pay such prices has public appreciation befallen these masters in the measure they deserve.

There is much talk about the absurdity of prices for the works of Millet, Rousseau, Barye and their contemporaries which is fallacious because based on an incomplete view of the situation. Putting aside the gigantic sums paid in consequence of rivalry at auctions, the amounts paid at private sales between cautious negotiators appear fabulous, especially when they are contrasted with the payments in the first instance made to the artist for the very same object.

But are they absurd, as commonly one hears them called? It is forgot that large sums of money are paid for canvases into which the smallest amount of talent enters, canvases that come from the studios of men who have been fashioned into skilled painters without possessing a gleam of genius or a throb of passion, or at any rate unable notwithstanding their perfected hand to communicate passion, feeling, emotion intellectual or emotion psychical to the onlooker. Works of this kind are and must always remain those which regulate the general prices of works of art in their own field. They are very high, far too high, if we are to believe the stern critics of mediocrities. But they establish a standard of price just as much as the bulk of wheat, corn and beef establishes in each case the general price for the necessities of life.

But now comes the rare artist who has something in his work that no Parisian training can supply if the genius is not there inborn and the circumstances under which he grows up are not fitted to ripen that genius. Only while his merits are understood by a comparative few can his pictures be sold below or on the same level with the clever work of mediocrities. As soon as the secret is in the possession of the wide world of buyers the price of his statuettes, paintings, water-colors or etchings tends upwards toward those 'ridiculous' sums against which we hear artists as well as amateurs declaim.

Let them call such sums ridiculous if they will. All I wish to say is that it is unphilosophical to regard them in that way, and even material. There is no price which is ridiculous for the plays of Shakespeare, the epics of Dante, the compositions of Beethoven, the paintings of Rembrandt. There is an angry note in comments on the great prices paid at present for works by the band of artists who have made France illustrious during the last half century. All that is wrong. One should glory in the fact that men are willing to pay a great fortune for a canvas a few inches square. There is no parallel between facts like these and the squandering by Romans of the value of huge properties on a banquet or one dish for a meal. The true parallel is with popular movements in ancient Greece and mediæval Italy when the advent of a work of art was the signal for a popular procession and ceremonies as important as if a conqueror returned in triumph.

Nor need we grieve that Barye got for his bronzes insignificant sums compared with those now asked for them. We should feel glad that the number of persons who recognize their beauty has increased so much that he obtains now that fame for which he labored. Barye longed for greater recognition when alive, but he also deliberately sacrificed a thousand chances for that recognition in order that his fame after death should be greater. His agony when creditors seized his models, his scrupulous care that no work below the best should leave the shop, his anxiety that a true amateur should possess the finest results of his genius and labor are warrant in saying this, not as a guess, but as an

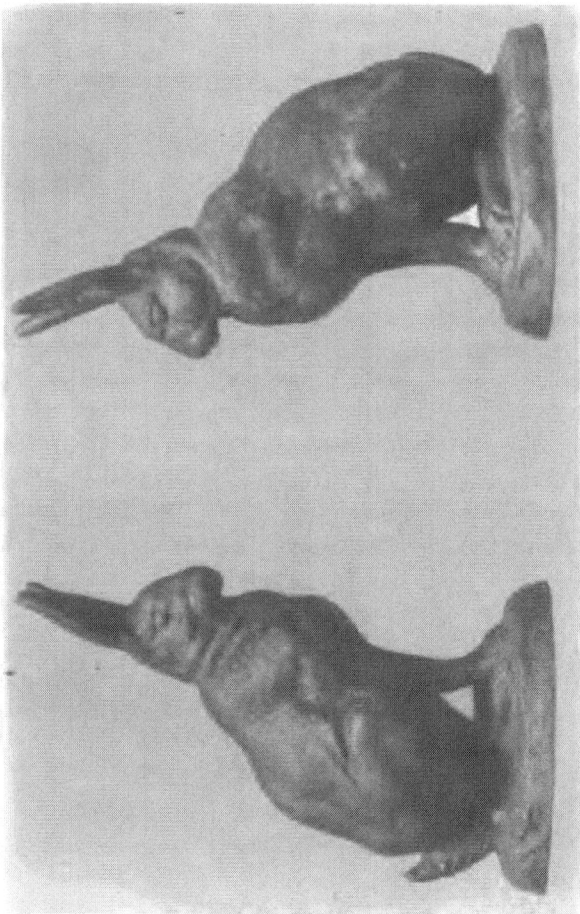

NO. 13.

SEATED HARE

Height 3 inches

indubitable fact. And there is this point in which the present day differs widely from former epochs when there was some truth in the complaint that men of giant fortunes absorbed the great products of sculptor and painter.

Nowadays fortunes are divided among heirs, and even before the millionaire dies the chances are great that his works of art are placed in some gallery where they are cared for as they could not be in ordinary hands, where they are protected from the dangers of fire and water and the wear and tear of transfer from owner to owner, and whither the public can come to examine them at their leisure. We must not be disgusted at the wide difference between the price of a Barye bronze in 1875 and in 1890. On the contrary it is a subject for congratulation that amateurs should think it worth their thousands to dispute a work of art among them. We have plenty of colossal monuments costing fortunes that have no spark of that genius we see in the minim bronze of a Seated Hare with ears erect stamped here on the back of the cover and found elsewhere in artotype. The architects of colossi are very apt to be pigmies in art. But Antoine Louis Barye when he modeled a pigmy animal was nothing less than an artistic giant.

CHAPTER SIX

I

LE PÈRE COROT was born the same year as Barye and oddly enough died at the very same age. Jean François Millet also died in 1875, so that France was bereft at once of three artists whose like we shall probably never see again. Daubigny followed in 1878 but Jules Dupré was living at the opening of the present year.

Of all the painters and sculptors whom Barye out-lived there was none who can be said to have influenced his career as an artist, except one who died as early in the century as 1826, namely Géricault the painter of the Raft of the Medusa, a man who died at the early age of thirty-three, but left behind him a most vivid impression on French sculpture as well as on French painting. He painted lions and tigers well, and his horses are often superior to those of Delacroix. Géricault was alternately soldier and artist and always a man of ill-regulated life. But while Barye was in his formative epoch this brilliant meteor rose on his horizon and captivated his senses.

Another who may have moved him for a time was Auguste Préault, a sculptor several years his junior who made his appearance and

130

NO. 85.

A. L. BARYE. PORTRAIT BY BONNAT

a sensation at the Salon at nearly the same period. It was in 1833 that Préault surprised the dignified sculptors of the old school with bas-reliefs and figures that were prophetic of Les Misérables by Victor Hugo, such as the figure of a young girl dying in the arms of her mother, and a colossal bas-relief called Famine. Préault in his early period seems to have been the Rodin of his day—unless it may be more logical to say that Rodin is the Préault of the present time It was he who remarked concerning the men opposed to his views of the proper scope of sculpture: 'Academicians are not artists; they are college ushers who have been promoted in rank.' In 1834 this tumultuous young artist created a yet greater sensation with a medal of an old Roman Emperor of most revolting countenance, and a bronze bas-relief called Slaughter. The latter was one jumbled mass of men, women and children destroying each other, and caused many persons to think it the work of a madman. Préault did some good and many poor statues later in the century, but his entrance of the Salon as a sensational sculptor of the first rank is mentioned merely to show that the terrible bronzes by Barye did not stand absolutely alone. Préault is now so forgotten that his existence as a sculptor is ignored in Siret's dictionary of artists. In 1824, nine or ten years earlier, Delacroix had made his mark with a Massacre of Scio, and in 1831, the year of Barye's first triumph, Delacroix showed amongst other things a painting of tigers.

So Barye was not separated entirely from the rest of the outside world either by the subjects he chose, or the dramatic feeling he showed in his animal groups. The difference between him and artists like Delacroix and Préault was that he controlled better his hand and studied more patiently the preliminaries to his groups. The result is that while Préault is as good as dead to the world of amateurs and Delacroix is rather losing ground than otherwise, Barye is continually growing in esteem and bids fair to take a position as regards Delacroix for example which would have been hardly considered possible by that ambitious and hard-working genius.

It is more than likely that to Barye his early friend Delacroix was at once a riddle and an object of veneration. Delacroix wrapped himself so closely in his work that he kept away from acquaintances and friends of youth, only frequenting certain aristocratic houses in the best quarters of Paris where his polished manners and cleverness made him most welcome. To be a colorist at that period was to be the bugbear of Academicians. Delacroix was a man of icy manners in society but a person full of fire and passion with regard to his work. The opposition of the conservatives in art merely deepened his anger and hardened his resolve to beat them sooner or later. Not only did he succeed in painting a great many ceilings and walls in the teeth of competition and intrigue, but he fought his way up through the steps of the Legion of Honor and into the august company of the Immortals. He was the hardest of all combatants to beat, a man who kept his temper outwardly and never showed discouragement under temporary defeat. When at last he wrested open the doors of the Institute the members of that body are said to have been not a little astonished to find him a delightful comrade who was polished naturally and in every way able to hold his own and contribute to their enjoyment.

Very different was the entrance of Barye. He was never a sociable man in the superficial way, and he gained his seat too late in life to change in any degree the habit of reserve and silence that characterized him.

It was not till five years after his death that M. Bonnat undertook for Mr. Walters a portrait of Barye in oils. It is seldom that this celebrated painter of portraits who rarely, if ever, makes an unsuccessful likeness and never a weak one is able to surpass his ordinary level so well as in this case. The artotype gives at least the firm, intelligent expression of Barye if it can not reproduce the values of the paint. Barye is remembered by Jules Clarétie in his Peintres et Sculpteurs Contemporains who gives a portrait etched by Massard which appeared in 1882.

It was not till the end of 1885 and the beginning of 1886 that an honor befell the memory of Barye such as lacks a parallel in modern

No. 82. PEACE, GROUP ON LOUVRE.
Stone.

times. One has to go back to the period of Greek art of the grand epoch and of Greek colonies to meet its like, for in that age a distant city would adorn itself and hold festival in order to greet the coming of a masterpiece by a sculptor of fame, or the monument erected to some great soldier or artist who lived and died in the motherland which had founded the city in question. The idea of traveling to America would have surprised Barye beyond measure, yet America has given him honors which France hopes at this late day to rival.

In February of 1886 the city of Baltimore was enriched with no less than five bronzes of large size, all of them after Barye's work. As already noted they were the gift of Mr. William T. Walters, who threw his collections of paintings, porcelains and bronzes open to the public and summoned from New York, Philadelphia and Washington a number of amateurs to rejoice with him over the American monuments to Barye. In his very interesting life of Barye M. Arsène Alexandre says: 'It is to Baltimore we must go in order to find a monument worthy of the artist. To build it his own masterpieces were enough, those which we neglect on the terrace of a public garden, or at an absurd height above portals where they are not seen. Thanks to the generous enthusiasm of Mr. Walters, a

No. 81.
WAR, GROUP ON LOUVRE.
Stone.

collector of the finest proofs known, the Lion in Repose and the four groups of the Carrousel Court are erected on one of the squares of Baltimore. The museum of Washington is equally rich in Barye bronzes, much richer than our national museum which possesses only two works by him.'

It is in the present year, however, that most has been done to spread the fame of Barye about the world. He has been raised in France to the number of those artists who are thought worthy of a place in the army of statues that people the city on the Seine. He has been thought in America a proper subject for one of those movements which are an honor to the memory of any man, whether the financial end sought thereby be attained or not, and a movement which is also sure, as we shall presently note, to do as much good on this side to the cause of native sculpture as it will prove on the other side of the Atlantic a graceful offering to a sister republic.

II

ADMIRERS of Barye in France conceived the idea of erecting a monument to him somewhere in Paris and that idea came to a tangible result in the spring of the present year. No better plan was outlined than a repetition of such an exhibition of works by Barye as occurred just after his death and the place chosen was the same, the École des Beaux Arts. It was urged that the Universal Exposition made such a design perilous, because all attention would centre on the Champs de Mars; but others held that among the floods of French and foreign visitors a certain number would remember Barye, and that even a fraction of so large a crowd would serve to increase the fund. The exhibition was accordingly held, and so far as first proof bronzes, models in bronze, clay, terra-cotta and wax are concerned none could have been more complete. Moreover there were plaster models of the great groups in stone at Marseilles and a hundred objects treasured by Barye's children and his particular friends which lend so much interest to a showing in the native place of an artist. Nevertheless financially speaking the exhibition was a failure. The flood of visitors set so powerfully toward that epitome of the world, the city reared just across the Seine from the Trocadéro, that no side rills found their way to the École des Beaux Arts. Instead of adding to the fund there was a deficit from the exhi-

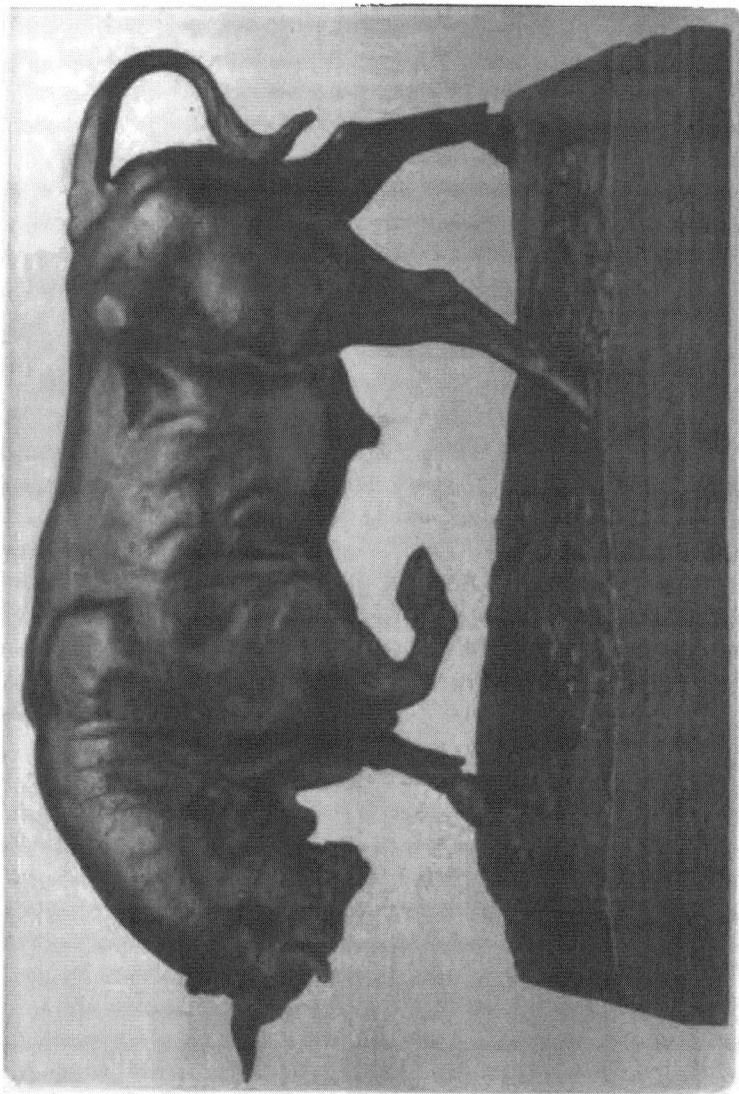

NO. 50.

BULL ON THE DEFENSIVE.

Height 7½ inches

bition of Barye's works. Thus by reason of the overwhelming interest of the great fair the small side show was forgotten.

Meantime the United States had taken so many of the bronzes, oils and water-colors of Barye that a suggestion for an exhibition in New York, at the same time with that in Paris, was very natural. It led to the formation of the Barye Monument Association, a list of whose officers will be found in the appendix, and the decision that an exhibition of works by A. L. Barye owned in the United States should be held in autumn at New York to collect funds for the monument to be erected at Paris. When the Paris exhibition closed the plaster cast of the Lion Crushing a Serpent shown there became available, and at the suggestion of Mr. George A. Lucas, the amateur of Barye bronzes, this was presented by the French Government to the Metropolitan Museum of New York, with the understanding that it should be exhibited first by the Barye Monument Association in autumn. The exhibition was duly opened on the 15th of the present month (November) at the American Art Galleries on Madison Square.

It has sustained comparisons very well with the objects shown in the spring at the École des Beaux Arts. In water-colors by Barye it is stronger. There are a score of bronzes here which were not represented in Paris, while about half that number constitute the specimens shown there which are not to be found here. No plaster models of the big groups in stone have reached America, though they were shown in Paris, and no such array of models in wax as was a distinguishing feature at the École. But there is everything necessary to make an exhaustive study of Barye and discover how great was the loss to the world when his powerful and fertile brain refused to guide his hand through the clay as it used to in the three decades 1830 to 1860. Surprising above all is the thought that America should have appreciated Barye so early and to such excellent effect as to have his works in bronze almost complete, although the taste for ornaments of the kind can be called in no sense national, and though the subjects of the bronzes are such as to make them particularly unattractive to the average American. By themselves these groups prove that there exists scattered through communities which at present are anything but educated to high artistic planes a great number of connoisseurs of fine quality who possess the true enthusiasm of the collector of works of art.

Concerning the masterpieces of painting by Jean François Millet, Eugène Delacroix, Théodore Rousseau, Corot, C. J. Daubigny, Troyon, Jules Dupré, Géricault, Decamps and Diaz de la Pena this is not the occasion to speak. It would be wrong, however, to ignore the presence of the better part of these comrades and fellow-strivers of Barye, that part of them which still lives on earth, because through these pictures their influence for good extends beyond the tomb and helps to build the monument to their friend. Were they alive, how gladly the greater number of them would contribute their pictures to an exhibition in such a cause! And now that they are dead the owners of their masterpieces feel the poetic fitness of such a bringing together of works by the immortal band who lived sparely and fought shoulder to shoulder through the Sacred Springtide of 1830. They are merely the custodians of these works and may well feel satisfied to employ them as their authors would have under similar circumstances.

There is yet another satisfaction to be felt in the exhibition of all these products of illustrious artists of France far away from the scenes where they were created—and a satisfaction that may occur to every American, whether he knows a Barye bronze from a fire-dog or a Millet landscape from a scene-painting. It consists in the fact that these men were citizens of a land which upholds in Europe the great principles for which our forefathers in America struggled. In this exhibition of French masters a republic more than oné hundred in age honors the republic which has lived for twenty years in seas far stormier than any we know in this part of the earth.

No. 47. GENERAL BONAPARTE.
Bronze. Height, 14 inches.

III

THE exhibition of Barye's bronzes in New York might easily be taken
for the whim of collectors of rare pieces of bric-à-brac by those who have
not studied, and also by those who understand perfectly their beauty as
works of art but have never considered the relation they bear to
sculpture in a much wider sense. From one point of view sculpture
that aims merely at the adornment of interiors may rightfully be
considered to stand on a lower plane than that which is intended for the
open air. Barye himself felt deeply the implied censure of his own
genius because his works were rarely permitted to address the moving
world of the streets and parks. But we must always keep well in
mind the axiom that art does not reside in magnitude. Barye's longing
to erect monuments of the largest size must not be interpreted to mean
that he undervalued his little bronzes. The care and genius displayed
in them attest that sufficiently. Though in the direction of large works
he was limited by want of appreciation, what he accomplished on the
scale suitable for the household has already had wide-spreading results
and will in future exercise a yet greater influence.

In this country even more than in France there is need of a change in
the view taken of the scope of sculpture. We have been accepting this
branch of the fine arts from Europe, but from the wrong end. We have
been aiming at the production of sculptors of the grand before growing
sculptors of the little, demanding from our artists large monuments
before we have learned by constant contact with small sculptures in our
households to understand what is really great in the art. It is exactly
as if we exacted from our painters the grandest of mural paintings
before we educated ourselves to appreciate such things by living with
easel work on our chamber walls. This has not been the process by
which we have evolved painters who are fit to take their place with the
best. These have been gradually brought forth by the agency of a
vast number of persons too modest to call themselves connoisseurs or

amateurs, who have bought etching and water-color and small painting as the taste grew and spread. The next step is now before us and our workmen are prepared for it. If the national government or a municipality, if a corporation or a rich citizen, ask now for mural work on a magnificent scale, the artists are ready to respond.

How different is the case of sculpture! Our exhibitions are devoted almost exclusively to the work of painters, etchers and engravers. The paucity of sculpture is too plain to be overlooked by the most careless observer. We are calling for battle monuments and elaborate statues to distinguished men, for pompous memorials to the dead in cemeteries, for sculpture to decorate the façades of enormous buildings. And when the sculptors do not supply us with statuary that equals in genius the best that France can evolve, we have an implied censure ready for them, a censure that necessarily penetrates beyond the artistic guild and returns upon ourselves, impugning the nation itself as one deficient in those flowers of genius whereby countries will be judged in the future. That blame falls rightly on us as a nation, but not for the reasons that are superficially assumed. The fault does not lie in a lack of artistic force in our mixed race. The fault lies in our crudeness, our ignorance. We have gone the wrong way about to attain that distinction in the arts which can only be won by an enlightened encouragement of sculpture.

We treat art as we treat religion. For six days it is forgotten and on the seventh it is taken up with an effort. Art like religion must be lived and breathed.

Barye's works point the way. Were that not so, certainly this book, a labor of love, would not have been written, and in all probability the exhibition for which it strives to serve as a memorial would never have been opened. For a group of collectors to work as faithfully and offer as generously the contents of their galleries as the case has been, there was need of something more than the barren honor of being exhibitors, more indeed than the praiseworthy endeavor to erect a monument to Antoine Louis Barye. The mainspring of the exhibition is the good that it may do the public by affording occasion for thousands

138

of men and women to realize what an important part sculpture on a small scale, so far as mere size is concerned, ought to play in our daily life. When that idea is thoroughly grasped the impulse to obtain fine specimens of bronzes by Barye, or Cain, or Mêne will be naturally transferred into the desire to own sculptures by native workmen. Then for the first time the art will begin to flourish from a healthy, sturdy root on American soil.

It is only necessary to examine the bronze, brass and iron work of our large buildings to see how low is the average of artistic force in the men who have modeled the designs. The spread of a taste for statuettes in the metals will effect a transformation downward and upward. It will make intolerable the barbarous shapes of gas-fixtures, lamps, grates, stoves, heaters and other necessities of modern interiors that are now treated in a spirit mistaken for art, but which would be far better if they had been left absolutely bare of ornament and bald. It will educate the average man who thinks at all about such matters to that point when he will not permit the erection on public places of such statues as disfigure all our cities, New York perhaps more than any other.

There is warrant for believing that this is not too much to expect from a popular encouragement of sculpture for the household and the fireside. We have only to reflect on the condition of the United States twenty years ago with respect to painting. Marvels have been done in the last score of years to educate the average man of mind with regard to pictures. What reason is there to despair of the republic so far as sculpture is concerned? After our collectors of foreign paintings had trained their eyes sufficiently a certain standard of excellence was indicated toward which it was necessary that native painters should approach at pains of being ignored should they fail to do so. Our painters accepted the conditions and every year show more plainly that they are worthy rivals of the very highest masters Europe can now show at work. Is it too much to claim that as soon as our collectors have learned to understand the charm of statuary for their homes by studying the work of men like Barye they will form in like manner a standard of

taste for such work, and ask of native sculptors that they shall approach
it? And if this takes place on a generous scale, as things commonly do
in our land, will not our sculptors respond as quickly and with as good
results as the painters?

The line of policy here marked out, to date from this exhibition of the
works of Barye, has the merit of following a tendency already apparent.
More and more every year the taste for sculpture is springing up. At
Boston, in New York, Philadelphia, Baltimore and at Washington, in
ten cities further to the west, the most visible signs are offered by the
public collections of casts from the antique. These indicate a groping
toward a revival of sculpture in the United States. The Barye
exhibition ought to do much in the way of clearing the minds of
amateurs on this subject. It is not enough to have such vast collections
of casts as that in the Metropolitan Museum under the Willard bequest.
Casts of beautiful small sculptures should be available in all our cities
for the adornment of interiors, the relief of external walls where protection exists from rain and snow, the decoration of offices private
and public. Taught by daily companionship with these cheap sub-
stitutes for the great creations of the sculptors of the past, the people
will of necessity advance to a demand for sculpture representing what
is about them, their relatives, friends and pets. Once the taste is formed,
a Barye, if such a genius is vouchsafed us, will not need to consume his
heart in bitterness because the public does not care for him and his
creations.

IV

MUCH more is to be said concerning Antoine Louis Barye, but the
rule that he who says everything becomes a bore remains today as true
as when it was uttered by the sly-faced philosopher of Ferney. There is
something pretentious in describing, explaining, commenting on works
of art when they are presented by wood-cuts and artotypes as fully as
they are here. Not that the artotype can do full justice to a Barye
bronze, let the photographer be ever so skillful, and the printer mix his

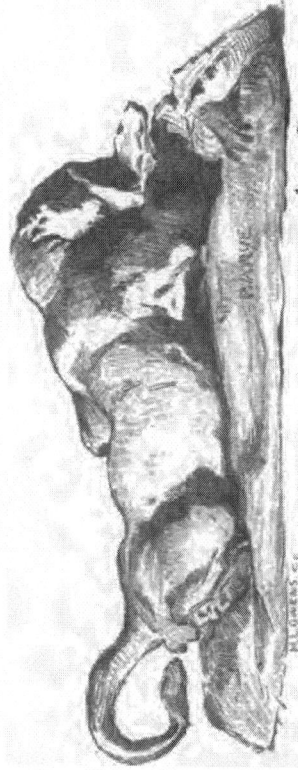

No. 44. JAGUAR SEIZING ALLIGATOR (rear).

Height, 8 inches.

inks with an eye ever so keen for shades of green, brown and gold. The variety of a bronze which has been treated by a master like Barye can not be translated in colors; only an approximation is possible. This is particularly the case when it has been in the possession of a lover of the arts, like Mr. George A. Lucas, to take but one instance. For the caresses that such a collector lavishes on a bit that pleases him, especially the rubbings here to bring out a golden high-light on a prominent muscle, the delicate brushings there to take dust out of a cranny without injury to the layer of green patina, produce an object that needs the hand of the most skillful painter of still life to render with exactness. Nor can any illustration give details which make all the difference between a statuette by Barye and one by another hand on the same theme.

The large complicated groups fare perhaps the worst; but in such an apparently simple thing as the statuette of General Bonaparte, how is an illustration to record the fact that the feet of Napoleon are not on a line, one leg being slightly farther forward in the saddle? And yet it is on just such little points as this that the beauty of the statuette depends. For one sees at a glance that the rider is at ease in the saddle; that in fact he is taking certain liberties with the correct seat of a soldier on horseback, and the impression that results is one of ease and mastery. One wood-cut cannot tell this. Nor would it be possible to show the beauty of another little equestrian statuette, that called L'Amazone, being a well-grown lady in the riding costume of 1830. The way she sits that horse! It is as easy as walking, and yet a riding-master might find fault with it in a fair beginner of the art of equestration. The whole figure of the woman is seen under the strong cloth. The stiff pomp of Gaston de Foix, clad in iron, astride his high saddle and the heavy horse that such fashions in war-clothes demanded, is much more easily given by an illustration. But how can the convolutions of the Python Surprising a Horseman be properly seen, unless the object itself is before one's eyes? Such as they are, these pictures nevertheless afford a better explanation than words can give. May the reader study them well and thank me for curbing the wish to expatiate on their various charms!

Chenavard the composer of cartoons for the Pantheon that treat of the world from Noah to the men of A. D. 4200 has left an orphic utterance as follows: *La haine est la vertu des brutes* — a remark that will not lose profundity on consideration. Its inner truth is particularly clear when we stand before a large gathering of bronzes by Barye of animals in conflict, and keep in mind the theory that every beast of the field, fish of the waters, bird of the airs, insect, tree and herb is what it is as the result of unnumbered ages of conflict. 'Hatred is the virtue of brutes' also implies that what is a virtue in them is a vice in us. Without that passion in beasts which assumes in our eyes the appearance of hatred there would be no evolution of horny plates on the alligator, of long sharp claws on the jaguar, of the stately head of horns on the stag and the shining tusks on elephant and boar. Under the grim mask of death that keeps all wild beasts and most wild men in a constant state of nerve-tension blooms the rose of progress and perfection, as we see on the quaint old tombstones in Haarlem Cathedral the blades of wheat growing up through an empty skull.

This fearful and yet fascinating department of thought Barye made his own and was the first to introduce into the arts. Let us thank him that he did not make the vulgar error of innovators and push realism to extremes. He enjoyed the terrible as do a vast number of people who have been taught to ask from art only the pretty and the conventional. He saw beauty in the terrible and perhaps felt that as an artist it was enough if he reflected in bronze that beauty without troubling himself about a deeper meaning. But the meaning was there and for his own pleasure and that of a very few others he thus increased tenfold the value of that which would have still been marvelous without it.

Chenavard was probably not prepared to spoil his epigram by extending it so far as to suggest that in man also hatred is a virtue, yet one of the awkward consequences of accepting evolutionary theories lies just

142

there. These passions which the wise of all ages have reprobated and religions denounced appear by analogy with the animal world to have done more than anything else to develop humanity. If we accept that as true we have to reconsider not only our relation to animals in general but the very basal ideas of morals and society. To meet this difficulty the champions of evolution maintain that the human race, although animal in origin, became by the development of the brain and hand so completely different from beasts that the analogies can no longer hold between the two. The lowest men who live and the lowest whose bones can be found in the earth are separated by a wide gulf from the highest of animals. If that be so, then Chenavard's maxim may stand for the brutes but need not apply to man.

Whichever way evolution be taken, whether we push the analogy so far as to include man, or stop in time to afford a chance for moralists to believe in evolution yet not surrender entirely their old position, there is this to comfort one in regarding Barye's works as so many scenes from the tragedy of the Struggle for Existence. We can be pretty certain that the stag beneath the claws of a panther, the horse on whose back a tiger has sprung, the doe enveloped in the folds of an anaconda, do not suffer half as much as we are prone to think. They are occupied with efforts to escape until a certain moment when they appear to lose sensibility. It may be doubted whether the carnivora do not suffer a hundred fold in captivity what they would if engaged in a hopeless combat with a stronger beast. The pleasure of battle would deaden them to anguish, just as a bull-dog does not know he is being torn. When a vital part is reached the wild beast feels nothing more. Human beings on the contrary suffer before and during a struggle owing to their imagination. If we keep this in mind we can regard with more equanimity the carnage suggested by the works of Barye, for they represent struggles which are by no means as terrible to the participants as they appear. At the same time this need not deaden us to the necessity of caring for animals and preserving them from unnecessary suffering, for when the special excitement of combat or struggle with an ancestral foe is absent, animals suffer in all probability a good deal more than we are disposed to believe, because of their limited means of expression and their habit of agonizing in silence.

V

BARYE presents us, to conclude this long disquisition, with a very remarkable instance of moral courage. When caste was much more important than it now is he never tried to conceal his humble position, as it appeared in men's eyes. He did not fail to sign objects that were nothing greater than paper-weights and decorations for clocks. His work as a jeweler caused him, like Benvenuto Cellini in 1568, to become *ardito di prendere a ragionare dell 'arte del oreficeria*, though he kept his processes of bronze work to himself instead of writing them down like the pugnacious Florentine. We see the results of his thought in his bronzes but have no word from him how he obtained such colors in the bronze. His bent was toward sculpture. Cellini in his eulogy on that art states that paintings often live only a few years, while sculpture is as it were eternal. But a natural tendency rather than arguments like this drove Barye to larger work. He has the credit of establishing again, as it was in Greece, and in Italy during the Renaissance, the art of sculpture on an equal footing with painting, not below it as exemplified in careless decorative pieces for the household, nor above it, as exemplified in great monuments, but hand in hand with painting as sculpture should go. With such a record we may well forget the hardships and disappointments of his career and fix our eyes on his triumphs and his achievements, feeling happy to remember that he lived all his life among great souls who acknowledged his worth and that his country did much if not everything to honor his genius.

DATES RELATING TO A. L. BARYE

A. D.

1791 The painter J. L. A. T. Géricault born at Rouen.

1793 Lyons partially destroyed by the army of the Convention from Paris.
Barye, a silversmith of Lyons, moves to Paris. Marries a daughter
of a lawyer named Claparède.

1796 Sept. 24th—Antoine Louis Barye born at Paris.
The painter J. B. C. Corot born at Paris.

1799 The painter Eugène Delacroix born at Paris.

1803 The painter A. J. Decamps born at Paris.

1805 Barye's education neglected.

1808 P. J. Chenavard born at Lyons.
Diaz de la Pena the painter born at Bordeaux.

1809 Auguste Préault the sculptor born at Paris.

1810 Barye apprenticed to Fourrier, engraver of military equipments.

1812 A. L. Barye drawn as conscript and placed in the brigade of topo-
graphical engineers, map-maker section.
The painters Théodore Rousseau and Jules Dupré born at Paris and
Nantes.

1813 Barye transferred to sappers and miners.
The painter Constant Troyon born at Sèvres.

1814 March. The army leaves Paris suddenly and Antoine Louis returns
home.
Apprenticed to the jeweler Biennais, makes the steel dies for stamping
repoussé work. Member of the National Guard.

1815 Jean François Millet the painter born at Gréville.
Barye finds a sculptor in his company of National Guards.

1816 Enters atelier of the sculptor Baron Bosio, a favorite of Napoleon.
1817 Enters atelier of Baron Gros the painter without leaving Bosio.
     C. F. Daubigny the painter born at Paris.
1819 Permitted to compete for the Prix de Rome at the Salon in the section
     of medals. Subject: Milo of Crotona Devoured by Lion. Prize to
     Vatinelle. Honorable mention to Antoine Louis Barye.
1820 Competes in the section of sculpture. Subject: Cain Hearing the Voice
     of the Almighty. Prize to Jacquot.
1821 Same section. Subject: Alexander Storming the Town of the Indian
     Oxydrakæ. Prize to Lemaire.
1822 Same section. Subject: Joseph's Bloody Garment Shown by his Brothers
     to Jacob. Prize to Seurre fils.
     E. Delacroix shows at Salon Dante and Virgil in Hell.
1823 Same section. Subject: Jason Bearing Off the Golden Fleece. No
     prize awarded.
     Enters workshop of Fauconnier, jeweler to the Duchesse d'Angoulême,
     Rue du Bac.
     Barye married and living in Passage Ste. Marie near his workshop.
     Industrial Exhibition. Fauconnier's exhibit contains models for
     making figures of animals.
1824 Not permitted to compete for the Prix de Rome.
     Delacroix shows in the Salon his Massacre of Scio.
     Barye models on his own account small animals, hunting dogs, bas-
     reliefs, which are cast by Tamisier.
1825 J. L. David the painter dies aged 77.
     Barye attends lectures on anatomy at the Zoölogical Gardens; reads
     Cuvier, Buffon, Lacépède, Lamarck. Studies archæology and fre-
     quents museums.
1826 Bas-reliefs: Eagle Exulting over Dead Chamois. Læmmergeyer and
     Serpent. Retriever and Duck.
     Géricault the painter dies aged 33.
1827 Sends to Salon: Bust of a Young Man. Bust of a Young Woman.
     Medallions.
     Delacroix the painter sends to Salon pictures of English and Turkish
     horses.
1828 Models and has cast small pieces:
     Stork, Tortoises, Stork on Tortoise, Rabbit, Hare.
     Elected to a dining club meeting at Mère Saguet-Bourdon's at the
     Barrière du Maine. Members: Béranger, Alexandre Dumas, Sainte
     Beuve, Chenavard, Abel Hugo, etc.
1830 Tiger Devouring Antelope or Gazelle, cast in bronze by the Galvano
     Plastic process.

1831 Bas-reliefs in bronze signed and dated:
      Genet-cat Dragging a Bird.
      Panther Walking. Leopard Walking.
      Virginia Stag Running, antlered. The same without horns.
     Sent to Salon:
      Tiger Devouring a Gavial (crocodile) of the Ganges which won a
         Second Medal and was bought by the Minister of the Interior for
         the Luxembourg; now at Louvre.
      A Group of Animals.
      Bear, a sketch in clay.
      Martyrdom of St. Sebastian, terra-cotta, full-length.
     Delacroix sends to Salon a picture of two tigers, study.
     Barye leaves Fauconnier the jeweler.
1832 Sent to Salon:
      Lion Crushing a Serpent, plaster.
     Unique bronze of same, small, given to the Minister of Interior.
     Distinguished by the Prince Royal, Duke of Orleans.
1833 Government buys Lion Crushing a Serpent.
     A. L. Barye made chevalier of the Legion of Honor.
     Aug. Préault the sculptor sends to Salon Misery, a young girl dying in her
        mother's arms. Gilbert Dying. Famine, colossal bas-relief.
     Barye sends to Salon:
      Dead Gazelle, a plaster study.
      Stag Pulled Down by two Scotch Hounds.
      Bear Overthrown by Three Mastiffs.
      Horse Struck by Young Lion, plaster.
      North American and Indian Bears Struggling.
      Bear of Alps.
      Asian Elephant.
      Russian Bear.
      Charles VI Frightened in the Forest of Le Mans.
      Horseman of the XVth Century; equestrian statuette.
      Bust of the Duke of Orleans.
      Lion, in plaster.
      Medallions in a frame.
1833 Sent to Salon water-colors:
      Two Peruvian Jaguars.
      Tiger Devouring Horse.
      Indian Panther.
      Two Cape Lions.
      Two Bengal Tigers.
      Panther of Morocco.

1834 Aug. Préault the sculptor sends to Salon:
    Medals: Old Roman Emperor. Young Roman Emperor.
    Bronze bas-relief: Butchery.
    Barye finishes for the Duke of Orleans the following groups, to stand on
    an *épergne* or *surtout de table* designed by Chenavard:
    Five principal groups:
      Hunt of the Tiger with Elephant (centrepiece).
      Hunt of the Lion with Buffaloes (long piece).
      Hunt of the Wild Ox (long piece).
      Hunt of the Bear (round piece).
      Hunt of the Elk (round piece).
    Four groups of Two Animals to surround the Centrepiece.
      Eagle and Bouquetin.
      Serpent with Bison or Gnu.
      Lion with Boar.
      Leopard with Doe.
    These nine pieces cast by the wax process (*à cire perdue*) by Honoré
    Gonon and his two sons.
    Duke of Orleans asks the jury of the Salon (made up from the Institute)
    to accept these pieces, but the jury refuses.
    The Duke appeals to Louis Philippe in vain.
    Barye sends to the Salon:
      Dead Gazelle, in bronze.
      Horse Surprised by Young Lion, in bronze.
      Elk Surprised by Lynx, plaster.
      Walking Elephant (wax process) for the Duke of Nemours.
      Panther and Gazelle. Bear, bronze.
      Bear in his Trough, bronze, for the Duke of Orleans.
      Various water-colors of animals.
    Barye makes an etching for the Musée du Salon de 1834 of A. Dumas.
1835 Salon refuses statues of Aug. Préault.
    Baron Gros drowns himself.
    Barye sends to Salon:
      Lion Holding Guiba Antelope.
    Makes for Lyons Museum:
      Tiger Devouring Virginia Deer, stone, colossal.
      The same, bronze reduction, for M. Thiers.
    Honoré Gonon and sons cast the Lion Crushing a Serpent by the wax
    process. Set up in the Avenue des Feuillants, Tuileries.
    Thiers suggests that Barye shall ornament the Place de la Concorde
    with groups; then the four corners of the Concorde bridge; then gives
    but does not confirm an order for a colossal lion.

1835 Thiers asks Barye for a design for the top of the Arc de Triomphe, Place de l'Étoile.

Barye models an Eagle, twenty meters from tip to tip of wing, alighting on trophies of war. Four Rivers, bound, to be placed at the four corners of the attic.

Design rejected for diplomatic reasons.

1836 Walking Lion.

Walking Tiger.

Sends to Salon various small bronzes which are refused.

Salon accepts:

Seated Lion (or Lion in Repose), plaster.

Barye casts by the wax process for the Duke of Orleans:

Elk Surprised by Lynx; unique piece given by the Duke to Alexandre Dumas.

1837 Sends nothing to Salon.

L'Amazone (Lady on Horse, Costume of 1830).

Recumbent Bear, plaster sketch.

Lion Devouring Doe, signed and dated, bronze.

Virginia Deer Scratching its Side, signed and dated, bronze.

Bull Pulled Down by Tiger.

Elephant Crushing Tiger, bronze for the Duke de Montpensier.

1838 Sends nothing to Salon.

Stag Listening, fore-feet together. Signed and dated.

General Bonaparte, equestrian statuette.

Receives order for Walking Lion, bas-relief on column of July, Place Bastille.

1839 Borrows money to set up a foundry and shop for statuettes in bronze.

Models in plaster Lion for July Column and Head of Cock for angles of same.

Charles VII the Victorious, equestrian statuette.

Gaston de Foix, equestrian statuette.

Speared Boar with mouth open.

Recumbent Bull Seized by Bear.

Panther with Foot on Muntjac Deer.

1840 Python Swallowing Doe.

Panther of Tunis Recumbent, signed and dated.

Python Crushing Crocodile.

Jaguar Standing, signed and dated.

Duke of Orleans, equestrian statuette.

Reclining Fawn, signed and dated.

Reclining Doe, signed and dated.

Roger Bearing Off Angelica on the Hippogriff, bronze for the Duke of Montpensier.

1840 Candelabra for the same, with Venus, Minerva and Juno, Three Graces, chimæras and masks as ornaments.
1841 Sends nothing to Salon.
Begins Theseus Slaying Minotaur.
Bull on the Defensive.
Bull Rampant.
Sleeping Fawn.
Small Seated Lion of different sizes.
1842 Nothing to Salon.
Foundry and shop do not pay.
Ape Riding Gnu.
Reclining Fawn etched by Ch. Jacque.
1843 Nothing to Salon.
Bear Flying from three Mastiffs. (Part of Bear Hunt.)
1844 Nothing to Salon.
Figure from Bear Hunt, a Huntsman with Quarterstaff, also called Mediæval Peasant.
Barye is commended by Thoré.
1846 Shop in Rue de Boulogne, Chaussée d'Antin.
Begins Lapith Slaying Centaur (called later Theseus Slaying Bianor).
Finishes Theseus Slaying Minotaur in bronze, and offers it for sale at his shop.
1847 Furnishes for the Pont d'Iena seven Eagles.
Lion Seated (or in Repose, begun 1836) is cast in bronze for the Quay Gate of Louvre, Pavilion de Flore, and placed on right as one enters.
Declines to make a duplicate for opposite jamb of gate on left.
Reversed duplicate cast and set up.
Jaguar Devouring Agouti (sketch for Jaguar Devouring Hare).
1848 Made by Ledru Rollin Curator of Plaster Casts at Louvre.
Jaguar Devouring Hare (now in Louvre).
Finishes Lapith Slaying Centaur.
Trimolet makes pen and ink portrait of Barye. Engraved by Ville-minot.
1849 Resides in Rue Ste. Anastase in the Marais.
1850 Jury of Salon no longer taken from the Institute but from artists.
Barye Sends to Salon (first time since 1836):
Theseus Slaying the Centaur Bianor (the same as Lapith Slaying a Centaur, slightly changed).
Jaguar Devouring Hare (plaster).
Minister of Interior buys Theseus Slaying Bianor; cast later in bronze; sent to the provincial museum at Le Puy.
Resides Rue des Fossés St. Victor.

APPENDIX

1851 Sends to Salon:
Theseus Slaying Minotaur (begun 1841, finished 1846).
Gustave Planche, in Revue des Deux Mondes, has an enthusiastic article on Barye; urges that his General Bonaparte, equestrian statuette, be erected size of life at the Invalides, Napoleon's tomb.
Resides Rue Montagne Ste. Géneviève.
Receives an order for ninety-seven Mascarons, decorations for the Pont Neuf.

1852 The sculptor Pradier dies.
Louis Napoleon takes the throne.
Barye sends to Salon:
Jaguar Devouring Hare, in bronze (shown 1850 in plaster).
Minister of Interior buys it for the Luxembourg collection, now in Louvre.
Loses Curatorship of Plaster Casts at Louvre.

1853 The widowed Duchess of Orleans sells the Table Ornaments of 1834.
Demidoff pays for Hunt of Tiger 4100 francs.
Demidoff pays for Hunt of Bear 7100 francs.
Lutteroth pays for Hunt of Wild Ox 4500 francs.
Montessier pays for Hunt of Lion 3000 francs.
Montessier pays for Hunt of Elk 4900 francs.
Gambard pays for Eagle and Bouquetin 1200 francs.
Béjot pays for Leopard and Doe 900 francs.
Hautpoeus pays for Serpent and Gnu 950 francs.
Hautpoeus pays for Lion and Boar 1005 francs.

1854 Lefuel succeeding Visconti as architect of the Louvre orders of Barye four groups to decorate inner façade of Louvre, Cour du Carrousel.
Barye models four groups of man, boy and beast, viz.:
Peace with Bull.
War with Alert Horse.
Force with Somnolent Lion.
Order with Subdued Tiger.
They are cut in stone; placed very high out of sight on the Pavilions Denon and Mollien.
Peace and War on Mollien.
Order and Force on Denon.
Cast the Theseus and Centaur in bronze.
Frémy and Joseph Decaisne procure an appointment for Barye as Professor of Drawing at the Jardin des Plantes.

1855 Shop at No. 10 Rue Saint Anastase, Marais, 113 bronzes for sale.
Universal Exposition.
Barye receives Grand Medal of Honor in the section of artistic bronzes.
Barye receives Officer's Cross of Legion of Honor.

1855 Bayle St. John calls attention to Barye's genius in ' The Louvre';
London : Chapman and Hall.
November. The sculptor Rude dies at the age of 71 years.

1856 Théophile Silvestre has an appreciative review of Barye as a sculptor and
a man in Histoire des Artistes Vivants, Français et Étrangers. Paris :
E. Blanchard ; Catalogues by L. de Virmont ; Portrait of Barye from
Daguerreotype on steel by Flameng.
Gustave Planche urges in print that Theseus Slaying Centaur Bianor at
the Le Puy museum be doubled in size, cut in marble and placed in
Tuileries.

1859 W. T. Walters of Baltimore becomes interested in Barye's bronzes, and
buys for presents and his own home.

1860 Wm. M. Hunt the painter induces Americans to buy bronzes.

1861 Richard M. Hunt, student of architecture, models animals at the Jardin
des Plantes under Barye.

1862 Equestrian Statue of Napoleon I for Ajaccio, Corsica.
A Victory for the same.

1863 Eugène Delacroix dies aged 64.
Barye made President of the Consulting Commission, Central Union of
Arts applied to Industries.
April 30th. Walking Lion in Solid Silver the Grand Prize at the Long-
champs races won by Fille de l'Air, owned by Count de la Grange.
Grand Clock for the Hôtel Pereire with Apollo Conducting the Chariot
of the Sun and Hours leading his steeds. Unique piece.
Sketches for portions of this :
Apollo as Sun-god Seated, plaster.
Apollo Standing, plaster.
Woman Standing, plaster.
Antique Chariot, plaster.

1865 Barye's studio is in the Rue Mouffletard.
Order received for an Equestrian Napoleon I for Grenoble.
The painter Constant Troyon dies.

1866 April. Barye hearing that Mercié had been asked for a design for the
Grenoble Napoleon throws up the commission.
Barye offers himself as candidate for Member of the Institute and is
refused.
Receives order for a bas-relief in bronze over entrance to Carrousel
Court of Louvre, Pavilion Lesdiguières : an equestrian Napoleon
III Dominating History and the Arts, triumphal piece in the Roman
style.
Also two Reclining River-gods, stone, for the same front.

APPENDIX

1866 Barye considered by Théophile Gautier in l'Illustration. Portrait by
      Mouilleron engraved on wood.
      Crayon sketch of Barye by Français.
      Bust and medallion of Barye by Geoffroy Dechaume.
      Barye carves in marble a Sainte Clotilde for a chapel in La Madeleine.
1867 Théodore Rousseau the painter dies aged 55.
      February. Article on Barye in the Gazette des Beaux Arts by Paul
      Mantz.
      Bust of Barye in bronze by Moulin.
      Carpeaux takes a pen and ink sketch of Barye.
      Exposition of 1867.
      Barye receives the Grand Gold Medal.
      Order for four groups at Marseilles.
      Barye models Jaguar Overthrowing an Antelope. Bear Overthrowing
      a Buck (fallow deer).
      These two sketches are put aside for other groups and are now owned
      by Barbédienne.
1868 Barye cuts in stone, colossal size, for the Château d'Eau at Marseilles:
      Tiger and Doe.
      Tiger and Fawn.
      Lion and Boar.
      Lion and Antelope.
      Barye is induced to offer himself once more to the Institute and is made
      Member of the Institute.
1869 Nereid Arranging her Necklace.
      Arab Riding on a Camel.
1870 Napoleon III, bas-relief on Pavilion Lesdiguières, Louvre, plastered
      over after Sédan and removed later.
1873 Declines an order for a grand vase with Centaurs and Lapiths in relief,
      stating that he might not be able to finish it.
      W. T. Walters, as Chairman of a Committee for the Corcoran Gallery,
      Washington, gives Barye an order for one of every bronze he has
      made.
1874 Barye supplies the Corcoran Gallery with 120 separate pieces.
1875 Corot dies aged 79.
      J. F. Millet dies aged 63.
      June 25. A. L. Barye dies aged 79, leaving a wife and eight children,
      with two daughters more by his first wife.
      Article in L'Art by A. Genevay.
      Article in L'Art by Ch. Blanc.
      Article in Journal des Débats by Clement.

1875 Military and popular funeral.

October. Exhibition of works at the École des Beaux Arts.

December. Sale of Barye's bronzes, models in wax and plaster, oils, water-colors and drawings at the Hôtel Drouot.

1878 C. F. Daubigny dies aged 61.

1880 Portrait in oils of Barye in old age painted by Léon F. Bonnat from photographs.

1882 Article by J. Clarétie in Peintres et Sculpteurs Contemporains, with etched portrait by Massard.

1885 February. W. T. Walters erects in Mt. Vernon Square, Baltimore, bronzes by Barbédienne after the following groups in stone on the Cour du Carrousel, Louvre :

Peace.

War.

Order.

Force.

Also bronze duplicate of the Seated Lion of the Quay gate of Louvre cast by Barbédienne.

September. Article by Theodore Child in Harper's Monthly Magazine, with fine wood-cuts by Kruell, Closson, F. French, Wolf, Muller, A. E. Wood, Faber, Bodenstab, Pettit, Tinkey, Wellington and Tietze.

1886 February. Article by Henry Eckford (C. de Kay) in The Century Magazine, with fine wood-cuts by Whitney, Turner, Schwarzburger and Kruell, after sketches by Kenyon Cox and W. H. Drake, and photographs.

February 27. Sichel Sale of Bronzes, etc. by Barye, at Paris; preface to the Catalogue written by Edmond de Goncourt.

1888 Proposition for a monument in Paris.

1889 April. Exhibition of Works by Barye at the École des Beaux Arts in aid of the fund for the monument. Notice in catalogue by Eugène Guillaume of the Institute, President of the Fund Association.

Life of Barye in French by Arsène Alexandre, published by Librairie de l'Art, Paris.

May. Article by Léon F. Bonnat on Barye in the Gazette des Beaux Arts.

Jules Dupré dies aged 77 years.

Plaster cast of Lion Crushing Serpent in the Tuileries Gardens presented by the French government to the Metropolitan Museum, Central Park, New York.

Suggestion from American admirers of Barye that something should be done to assist fund for his monument in Paris.

April. Organization discussed in New York.

APPENDIX

1889 May. At Baltimore, Md., a Barye Monument Association formed for
the United States with the following officers:
President: Wm. T. Walters.
Vice-Presidents: Cyrus J. Lawrence.
     Henry G. Marquand.
     James C. Welling.
Treasurer: Cyrus J. Lawrence.
Secretary: Charles de Kay.
Auditors: Thomas B. Clarke.
   Theodore K. Gibbs.
   Harry Walters.
Publication Committee: Alex. W. Drake.
       W. M. Laffan.
Managers of the Exhibition: American Art Association.
November. Exhibition at the American Art Gallery, 6 East 23d Street,
New York, of first proof bronzes, models in bronze, plaster and wax,
Barbédienne bronze reproductions, oils, water-colors and drawings by
Antoine Louis Barye owned in the United States; also of oil-paintings
by his friends and contemporaries, as follows:
Corot.   Daubigny, C. J. Decamps. Delacroix.
Dupré, Jules. Géricault.   Millet. Rousseau, Théodore.
       Troyon.
Catalogue by Cyrus J. Lawrence, with extracts from an article on Barye
by Léon F. Bonnat prefixed.

DRAUGHTSMEN, ENGRAVERS AND PRINTERS

FRONTISPIECE............................*Engraved on steel by Flameng*

TITLE-PAGE........................*From the drawing by W. H. Drake*

4 TIGER COUCHANT................... ....*Engraved by C. Schwarsburger*

5 ROCKS AT FONTAINEBLEAU ....*Engraved by W. H. Turner*

9 RABBIT ON THE ALERT }
10 RABBIT ON THE ALERT } .. ..*Drawn by Kenyon Cox*

16 TIGER DEVOURING GAVIAL.. .... *Engraved by John Tinkey*

19 A. L. BARYE AT 35 .... *Engraved by G. Kruell*

23 TIGER ROLLING...... .... *Engraved by Juengling*

24 LION CRUSHING A SERPENT .. ..*Engraved by Henry Marsh*

26 INDIAN AND AMERICAN BEARS ....*Engraved by John Tinkey*

27 STANDING BEAR. .... *Engraved by Louis Faber*

33 LION MEETING PYTHON.... ....*Engraved by W. B. Closson*

34 HUNT OF THE TIGER ...._...... .... *Engraved by Frank French*

40 EAGLE ALIGHTING ....*Drawn by W. H. Drake*

43 JAGUAR SEIZING ALLIGATOR }
44 JAGUAR SEIZING ALLIGATOR } .... *Drawn by Kenyon Cox*

45 FAWN AT REST...................................*Engraved by Cullen*

47 GENERAL BONAPARTE . ...*Engraved by David Nichols*

57 SEATED LION ....*Engraved by Miss C. A. Powell*

58 PANTHER DEVOURING AN AGOUTI.......... .... .*Engraved by F. A. Pettit*

59 JAGUAR DEVOURING A HARE...... ....*Engraved by Henry Wolf*

60 THESEUS SLAYING THE CENTAUR.. .... *Engraved by J. H. E. Whitney*

61 HEAD OF SEATED LION }
62 HEAD OF SEATED LION } .. .. *Engraved by W. B. Closson*

63 HUNT OF THE TIGER .... *Engraved by F. H. Wellington*

64 THESEUS SLAYING MINOTAUR ....*Engraved by J. H. E. Whitney*

65 BRONZE BUST OF BARYE............. . ...*Engraved by R. G. Tietse*

66 HUNT OF THE BEAR ....*Drawn by Kenyon Cox*

70 A. L. BARYE WITH CENTAUR GROUP ....*Engraved by G. Kruell*

73 LION IN SOLID SILVER .... *Engraved by A. E. Wood*

78 THE SEINE . ...*........ *Engraved from the bronze by R. A. Muller*

81 WAR ... ... *Drawn by Kenyon Cox*

82 PEACE ....`.... ....*Engraved by F. H. Wellington*

83 ORDER .. .. }
84 FORCE............ } . ... *Drawn by Kenyon Cox*
86 ELEPHANT RUNNING }

FRONTISPIECE...... ....*Printed by Kimmel & Voigt*

WOOD-CUTS ON INDIA PAPER... .. ..*Printed by John C. Bauer*

WOOD-CUTS ON HOLLAND PAPER ......*Printed by Theo. L. De Vinne & Co.*

ARTOTYPES ....*Printed by Edward Bierstadt*

HEADBANDS AND TAILPIECES ... .*Drawn by Geo. W. Edwards*

ILLUSTRATIONS

No.			PAGE
1	A. L. Barye aged about 60	*Steel print* ..	Frontis-piece.
2	Walking Lion.. 1836	. *Wood-cut* ..	Title-page.
3	Walking Tiger 1836	. *Artotype*. ..	2
4	Tiger Couchant (water-color).....	*Wood-cut* ..	4
5	Rocks at Fontainebleau (oils)	*Wood-cut* .	6
6	Stork on Tortoise 1824	*Artotype*. .	8
7	Læmmergeyer and Serpent 1824	. *Artotype*....	10
8	Milo of Crotona Killed by Lion 1819	. *Artotype*. .	12
9	Rabbit on the Alert (rear)	*Wood-cut* ...	12
10	Rabbit on the Alert (side)..	*Wood-cut* ..	12
11	Seated Cat 1827	. *Artotype* ...	108
12	Dromedary of Egypt.. 1827	*Artotype*	14
13	Seated Hare (two views)	*Artotype*	128
14	Buck of Fallow Deer Playing with Stone 1830	*Artotype* .	16
15	Red Deer of Europe. Hart, Hind and Fawn 1832	*Artotype* .	16
16	Tiger Devouring Gavial of Ganges . 1831	*Wood-cut*	18
17	Stag Seized by Cougar (etching by Barye).	. *Wood-cut*	20
18	Ocelot and Heron	. *Artotype* ...	22
19	A. L. Barye at 35; after a lithograph by Gigoux 1831	. *Wood-cut* ...	24
20	Hart Seized by two Scotch Hounds . . 1833	. *Artotype* ...	26
21	Elephant of Asia Running 1834	*Artotype* ..	28
22	Horse Surprised by Young Lion 1833	.. *Artotype* ..	30
23	Tiger Rolling (water-color)	.. *Wood-cut*	32
24	Lion Crushing a Serpent; Tuileries. ... 1832	*Wood-cut* . .	34
25	Lion Striking at Serpent.	*Artotype*....	36
26	American and Indian Bears Wrestling . .. *Wood-cut* .. .		38
27	Standing Bear 1833	*Wood-cut* .	40
28	Barye Caricatured as a Bear	*Artotype*. ...	42
29	Bear Overthrown by Mastiffs 1833	*Artotype* . .	44
30	Bear in its Trough 1834	*Artotype* .	44

					PAGE
31	Bear Surprising Owl	....	..	Artotype. ..	46
32	Elk Surprised by Lynx	1834	..	Artotype.....	48
33	Lion Meeting Python Snake (water-color)	....	..	Wood-cut	126
34	Hunt of the Tiger	1834	..	Wood-cut	50
35	Hunt of the Elk	1834	..	Artotype.....	52
36	Hunt of the Bear	1834	..	Artotype.....	54
37	Hunt of the Wild Ox	1834	.	Artotype	56
38	Panther Devouring Gazelle	1834	.	Artotype.....	58
39	Panther of Tunis Couchant	....	.	Artotype.....	124
40	Eagle Alighting	1835	.	Wood-cut	60
41	Wolf Caught in Trap	....	..	Artotype. ..	62
42	Lion Devouring Doe	1837	..	Artotype.....	142
43	Jaguar Seizing Alligator (front)	1837	..	Wood-cut	66
44	Jaguar Seizing Alligator (rear)	1837	..	Wood-cut	140
45	Fawn at Rest (etching by C. Jacque)	1840	..	Wood-cut	62
46	Asian Elephant Crushing Tiger	1837	..	Artotype.....	70
47	General Bonaparte	1838	..	Wood-cut	136
48	Bull Attacked by Bear	1839	..	Artotype.....	64
49	Python Swallowing Doe (two views)	....	.	Artotype ..	122
50	Bull on the Defensive	1841	..	Artotype	134
51	Lion of the July Column, Place Bastille	1840	..	Artotype	112
52	Ape Riding a Gnu	1842	..	Artotype.....	68
53	Roger Bearing off Angelica on the Hippogriff	1840	..	Artotype.....	70
54	Candelabrum with Three Goddesses	1840	..	Artotype.....	70
55	Mediæval Peasant (from Bear-hunt)	....	..	Artotype. ...	118
56	Python Crushing a Crocodile	1840	..	Artotype.....	110
57	Seated Lion, Quai du Louvre	1846	..	Wood-cut	74
58	Panther Devouring an Agouti	1847	..	Wood-cut	76
59	Jaguar Devouring a Hare	1848	..	Wood-cut ..	90
60	Theseus Slaying the Centaur Bianor	1850	..	Wood-cut ..	78
61	Head of Seated Lion (front)	.	..	Wood-cut	86
62	Head of Seated Lion (profile)	....	..	Wood-cut	86
63	Hunt of the Tiger (from right)	....	..	Wood-cut ..	78
64	Theseus Slaying Minotaur	1851	..	Wood-cut	80
65	Bronze Bust of Barye by Moulin	1851	..	Wood-cut	82
66	Hunt of the Bear (another view)	1851	..	Wood-cut	XII
67	Panther Seizing Elk	1851	..	Artotype.....	84
68	Mounted Arabs Killing Lion	....	..	Artotype.....	88
69	Python Crushing African Horseman	.. .	..	Artotype.....	120
70	A. L. Barye with Centaur Group	....	..	Wood-cut	92
71	Tatar Warrior Checking Horse	....	..	Artotype.....	94

ILLUSTRATIONS

					PAGE
72	GREYHOUND AND HARE		..	*Artotype*	96
73	WALKING LION IN SOLID SILVER	1863	..	*Wood-cut*	98
74	WAR, STONE GROUP ON LOUVRE	1855	.	*Artotype*	100
75	PEACE, STONE GROUP ON LOUVRE	1855	..	*Artotype*	100
76	ORDER, STONE GROUP ON LOUVRE	1855	..	*Artotype*	102
77	FORCE, STONE GROUP ON LOUVRE	1855	..	*Artotype*	102
78	THE SEINE: LEFT-HAND RIVER-GOD, LOUVRE	1865	..	*Wood-cut*	106
79	AUTOGRAPH LETTER, BY A. L. BARYE	1866	..	*Artotype*	104
80	GROWLING WOLF WALKING (Rousseau's)		..	*Artotype*	116
81	WAR, STONE GROUP ON LOUVRE	1855	..	*Wood-cut*	133
82	PEACE, STONE GROUP ON LOUVRE	1855	..	*Wood-cut*	132
83	ORDER, STONE GROUP ON LOUVRE	1855	..	*Wood-cut*	160
84	FORCE, STONE GROUP ON LOUVRE	1855	..	*Wood-cut*	VIII
85	A. L. BARYE, PORTRAIT BY BONNAT	1875	..	*Artotype*	130
86	ELEPHANT OF SENEGAL RUNNING			*Wood-cut*	22

No. 83.
ORDER, GROUP ON LOUVRE.
Stone.

1053768R0

Printed in Great Britain by
Amazon.co.uk, Ltd.,
Marston Gate.